Mobility 3.0

How to Win and Thrive in the Future of Passenger Transportation

Leonardo Gannio

MOBILITY 3.0
How to Win and Thrive in the Future of Passenger Transportation

November 2024

Written by Leonardo C. Gannio

Dedication

To my wife, Fabricia

My daughters, María Sofía and María Lucila

My sisters, Flavia and Florencia. My parents, who, for sure, are inspiring me from somewhere in heaven.

And all the people who helped me shape my character, resilience, grit, professional career, and startup endeavors.

Acknowledgment

Writing a book can never be taken as an independent task. Instead, it is a long journey that requires extensive research, introspection, and teamwork. I am deeply indebted to all the following people who helped me realize this book. Hence, now is the opportunity to express my deep appreciation.

First and foremost, the personal mentors and industry experts who gave so much time and effort to provide valuable insight and advice along this process should be thanked. Their input into issues and viewpoints has been invaluable in deciding what this book would contain and in which directions it would move.

Their willingness to share their knowledge and engage in thought-provoking discussions added weight to the narrative and deepened the analysis. I am particularly indebted to my customers and friends, whose encouragement and critical inputs were indispensable in realizing this book's main ideas. Their continued encouragement has enthused and motivated me to complete this work.

I would like to appreciate the input of colleagues and fellow professionals. Their support, feedback, and critical reviews were integral in finalizing the manuscript. These colleagues brought into the project a cooperative spirit and intellectual rigors that have immensely improved the book's quality.

Thanks to the inspirational life example of my friend, Jean Maggi, who taught me that *"Everything is Possible,"* and his saying that is always a part of my life, *"The difficult thing is done, the impossible is attempted."*

I am grateful to my colleagues and peers' insightful reviews, which enhanced the text's clarity and coherence. These individuals have been invaluable in this entire period of writing and revising for their unending commitment and dedication.

I thank all my family, friends, and investors for their support and patience. Writing a book for publication is demanding and requires sacrifice; hence, their understanding and encouragement kept me going. I am incredibly grateful to my family and friends for always believing in me and for the much-needed emotional support in overcoming the hardships. Their patience and understanding have constantly reminded me to persevere and be dedicated.

Lastly, I would like to thank the readers and future passenger transportation leaders. I hope that the discussions and ideas across this book will inspire and empower you to be a driving force for positive change in your respective field. With everything going on in transportation today, it is time for the innovations and insights reviewed here to spur thoughts, motivate exploration, and invite a forward-looking mindset. The concepts and strategies outlined in this book show how visionaries passionately shape mobility's future.

This book has been a collective product. Therefore, I must express my deep gratitude to all who helped me toward the completion of this manuscript. Your support, guidance, and encouragement have been meaningful to me and my achievement. Thank you for sharing this journey and helping to bring these ideas to life.

About the Author

Born in Buenos Aires, Argentina, Leonardo Gannio is a seasoned industrial engineer with a rich educational background, including a postgraduate degree from IAE and executive courses at Stanford University. Over the years, Leonardo has demonstrated exemplary leadership in various multinational corporations such as NCR, Informix Software, PeopleSoft, and Ingram Micro, where he played pivotal roles in shaping corporate strategies and enhancing operational efficiencies.

Leonardo is an astute entrepreneur who founded and led multiple successful ventures across diverse sectors. He established *Inventika Solutions* in digital marketing, quickly becoming a leader due to its innovative approaches and robust service offerings. He launched *FixIt Urban Hardware Stores* in retail, a chain that redefined hardware shopping in urban settings.

His foray into technology distribution resulted in the *AKTIO Group*, which has grown substantially under his guidance, achieving revenues of $500 million and establishing a presence in seven countries across the Americas. Most recently, he ventured into the mobility industry with *MAGIIS,* an innovative platform that promises to transform urban mobility dynamics.

Leonardo's ventures are marked by a keen focus on technology and innovation, continually setting benchmarks in every industry he enters. His visionary leadership and relentless pursuit of excellence continue to drive his ventures to new heights, making him a prominent figure in the international business community.

Preface

The concept of mobility has always fascinated me. For most people, it's about getting from point A to point B, but for some of us, it's a deeper journey: a struggle against adversity, a testament to the strength of human will, and a canvas on which we paint our dreams. I have challenged the highest mountain range on the planet (the Himalayas) and the longest (the Andes), traveled across all continents, and defied what many believed to be impossible—not just because I wanted to move but because I wanted to prove that anything is possible.

When I think about the future of mobility, I envision a world without barriers, where technology and innovation create freedom for everyone, regardless of their circumstances. My friend, Leonardo Gannio, the visionary behind this book, is at the forefront of this revolution. His work in *"Mobility 3.0"* is about changing how we move, improving access, promoting equity, and unlocking economic opportunities for communities worldwide.

Mobility 3.0 is more than a technical evolution; it is a social movement that seeks to dismantle the physical, economic, and social barriers that have long limited people's potential. Imagine a future where mobility is no longer a privilege reserved for a few but a right accessible to all, where everyone, whether facing physical challenges or economic limitations, can move freely and confidently. This vision goes beyond personal freedom; it drives economic development by connecting people to jobs, education, and opportunities that were previously out of reach.

Leonardo's vision, outlined in this book, is the blueprint for this new world. It doesn't just predict the future of mobility; it actively shapes it, advocating for a collaborative ecosystem that prioritizes user experience, enhances access, and fosters equitable growth. From autonomous vehicles to Mobility-as-a-Service, Leonardo's insights offer a roadmap toward a future where every journey—whether on foot, on wheels, or in a vehicle—is smooth, sustainable, and inclusive.

Mobility 3.0 represents an opportunity to redefine our cities, reimagine our economies, and create a more just society. By leveraging technology, we can drive economic growth, reduce inequalities, and empower individuals and communities to thrive. This is more than just movement; it's about building pathways to a better life.

I am proud to contribute to this prologue because, like Leonardo, I believe in a future where movement is not a privilege but a right. *"Mobility 3.0"* is more than a book; it's a call to action. It's a challenge for every entrepreneur, policymaker, and innovator to dream big, break barriers, and create a world where freedom of movement knows no limits and economic opportunities are accessible to all.

Let's build a future where everyone, regardless of their abilities, can conquer their own Himalayas and where the journey toward equitable access and economic development is one we take together.

I always say in my public presentations that movement is magical, and *Mobility 3.0* proposes movement for all. A supreme magic.

Jean Maggi

Limitless Dreamer

https://jeanmaggi.com/en/bio-ingles/

Contents

Chapter 1
Introduction: Setting the Stage for the Future of Mobility and Why It Matters

In the enchanting embrace of a warm, oceanside afternoon on the Bay, a transformative narrative began to unfold. This region, renowned for its labyrinthine waterways and lush scenery, served as an unlikely backdrop for the birth of a revolutionary idea in transportation. My friend John and I were not urban planners; we were simply two friends enjoying the simplicity of a leisurely day away from the city's hustle.

As we navigated the calm waters of the Bay in a small, rented boat, our conversation naturally drifted toward the state of the mobility industry. Both of us had experienced the frustrations of daily commutes in congested cities—hours spent in traffic, the environmental toll of excessive carbon emissions, and the sheer inefficiency of it all. Surrounded by the laughter of friends and the rustle of the ocean, unbeknownst to us, we planted the seeds of a profound idea destined to revolutionize the realm of people's mobility. In this context, these seeds began to take root amidst the gentle rustle of ocean waves.

From that revelatory day on the Bay, it's pivotal to recall the historical significance of 22 December 2015, when another transformative chapter of my life began. Four months before that idyllic afternoon, I had inked a monumental agreement to sell my brainchild—a tech distribution company I founded in 2001 that had grown to extend its technological tendrils across seven Latin American countries, generating a robust revenue of $500 million.

The negotiation process to sell the company was grueling, stretching over eight months. This period was marked by intense pressure, countless meetings, and strategic maneuvering, demanding a deep reservoir of patience and resilience.

These negotiations were not merely business transactions; they were a profound learning journey, each session a lesson in economics, human psychology, and corporate strategy. As the final papers were signed and the company transitioned to new ownership, I also transitioned professionally and personally.

This sale was not just an end but a beginning. The closure of this chapter in my professional career marked the initiation of a new phase. With the sale's completion, I transplanted my life and my family to the United States to shepherd the acquired company as an executive. This move was both a professional requirement and a personal choice, offering new challenges and opportunities.

However, amidst this whirlwind of change, I found an unexpected solace during my visits back home. On one such visit, surrounded by the familiar laughter of lifelong friends and the comforting rustle of the Bay's waters, the seeds of a new idea began to sprout. The contrast between my life in bustling, high-stakes business environments and the serene simplicity of the Bay was stark. In the quiet of nature, away from the world's noise, my mind found the peace necessary to think creatively and boldly.

The idea born that day was not a sudden revelation but a culmination of experiences gathered over years of building a tech distribution conglomerate and navigating complex markets. It was fueled by the desire to integrate the technological prowess I had honed with a sustainable, efficient approach to mobility—a vision to use advanced technology not just for profit but for progress.

Reflecting on my journey, from founding a company that connected technology across continents to envisioning a future where technology connects people in cleaner, more efficient ways, I realized that my personal and professional transformations were deeply interconnected. Each phase of my life provided critical insights that were now converging into this new venture.

This book, therefore, is not just a technical manual for future mobility. It is also a narrative of personal growth, a tale of how transformative moments in life can lead to revolutionary ideas in business. It is about harnessing the wisdom gained from past experiences to innovate and lead in an ever-evolving world.

Continuing from that reflective narrative, it became increasingly evident during my subsequent visits home that the mobility industry, much like my previous ventures, was on the brink of significant transformation. This realization crystallized during one of the many animated exchanges I shared with John, my longtime friend, and a seasoned entrepreneur with extensive experience in the passenger transportation sector.

John had built his business from the ground up, starting as the sole proprietor driving his vehicle. Over two decades, he nurtured this venture into a substantial fleet of nearly 100 vehicles. His company's success was rooted deeply in a loyal customer base that valued the trifecta of safety, quality, and personalized service—all offered at a fair price. However, despite his accomplishments, John was considering an investment that seemed, at least to me, a step backward. He wanted to modernize his company's transmission antenna to broaden the reach of his vehicle dispatch center via VHF radio, which was confined to a mere 25-mile radius due to the existing antenna's limitations.

"Why invest in technology on the cusp of obsolescence, John?" I asked, genuinely curious about his rationale.

Although successful, his company was operating with technology that was rapidly becoming outdated. The passenger transportation sector was on the cusp of a technological revolution with the rise of digital and mobile platforms, and here was John, contemplating an investment in an old system.

"It's what I know which has yielded highly successful results for the last 25 years. So, why change now?" John responded.

His answer was simple yet profound, highlighting a common predicament many traditional businesses face adopting new technologies in a changing landscape.

This conversation with John served as a catalyst, sparking a deeper contemplation on the broader trends reshaping the passenger transportation sector globally. While John's approach had served him well in the past, it was clear that the industry was moving toward more advanced, integrated, and sustainable solutions. Technologies such as GPS tracking, mobile ticketing, real-time data sharing, and eventually, autonomous driving were set to redefine what was possible in transportation. Moreover, with electric vehicles and smarter urban planning, the shift toward sustainability promised to alter the mobility industry framework dramatically.

The dialogue with John made me think about the countless other entrepreneurs and small business owners in the passenger transportation sector who might be equally unaware of or resistant to these changes. This was a pivotal moment; it underscored the need for a guide that could bridge the gap between traditional operational methods and the forthcoming wave of technological innovation.

Eureka!

In that moment, a revelation unfolded. Before me stood John, a thriving entrepreneur in a burgeoning industry, yet one oblivious to the seismic shifts that could metamorphose the trajectory of his company. It was clear that while John's business acumen had brought him success, the digital transformation of the mobility industry could either elevate his enterprise to new heights or leave it struggling in the wake of progress. This realization was profound for the implications it held for John and countless other entrepreneurs operating within this space.

Thus, this book takes its inaugural breath—a chronicle of the journey that birthed my latest venture, MAGIIS, and the transformative potential within the mobility industry. This narrative is crafted to guide millions of entrepreneurs navigating the complexities of the passenger transportation sector daily, offering recommendations and a roadmap to thrive in a future prosperous with opportunities in the new digital economy.

The shift toward a digital economy in mobility is not merely about adopting new technologies; it's about a fundamental transformation in how passenger transportation services are conceptualized, delivered, and experienced. Entrepreneurs must understand that this shift is pervasive, influencing customer expectations, operational efficiencies, business models, and open ecosystems. Digital platforms, data analytics, artificial intelligence, and machine learning are not just tools but foundations upon which the future of mobility will be built.

This book aims to demystify these technologies and present them as accessible levers of growth that can drive significant value for businesses. It will delve into practical strategies for integrating advanced technologies to enhance customer engagement analytics, better understand customer patterns, optimize routes, reduce operational costs, and increase vehicle productivity through autonomous interaction with open ecosystems in the mobility industry.

It will explore how vehicle electrification, autonomous technology, Internet of Things (IoT) devices, personalization, and online communications can enhance vehicle maintenance, improve safety, and create a seamless passenger experience. Moreover, it will discuss the strategic importance of sustainability and how adopting green technologies is an ethical choice and a competitive advantage in an increasingly eco-conscious market.

The narrative will also emphasize the importance of agility in business strategy. The ability to adapt quickly to changing technologies and consumer preferences is critical. It will guide entrepreneurs through iterative development and continuous learning, encouraging them to experiment and innovate while managing risks intelligently.

The book will frame these discussions by recognizing entrepreneurs' challenges transitioning from traditional business models to digital-first approaches. It will respect the hard-earned successes of traditional methods while passionately advocating for adopting new strategies that promise greater efficiency and connectivity.

Concepts like Abundance versus Scarcity thinking models in the mobility industry will help entrepreneurs reshape their current companies to embrace the new digital economy while adopting advanced technologies, retrain their workforce focus on customer experience, and establish adequate KPIs (Key Performance Indicators) to foster an abundance tribe while achieving a doubtless success in the region where they operate (Countrywide or worldwide).

Furthermore, this transformation is not merely technological but also cultural. There is a growing expectation among consumers for services that are not only efficient but also sustainable and ethically managed. This shift pushes the industry toward electric vehicles and hybrid models, reducing the carbon footprint and aligning with global efforts to combat climate change.

In this context, my discussion with John becomes a microcosm of the more significant industry-wide shift. It illustrates the critical need for traditional business owners in the passenger transportation sector to embrace change, think beyond the conventional, and prepare for an increasingly digital, interconnected, and sustainable future.

In conclusion, the purpose of this book is not merely to predict the future of mobility but to actively shape it by empowering entrepreneurs with the knowledge, tools, and perspectives needed to succeed in the digital age. It seeks to inspire a proactive embrace of change, encouraging leaders in the mobility industry to not just participate in the digital economy but to lead it.

Thus, this book aims to serve as a comprehensive guide for current passenger transportation providers. It seeks to outline clear, actionable strategies that help bridge the technological and conceptual gaps that many traditional operators face. By doing so, it hopes to equip them with the knowledge and tools necessary to thrive in a rapidly evolving market, ensuring they are not only participants but leaders in the future of mobility.

Here's to navigating the new digital economy with insight, innovation, and integrity. Let us step boldly into this exciting future together, driven by the shared commitment to transform mobility for a better tomorrow.

Chapter 2
Finding Your 'Why':
The Strategic Edge for Mobility Providers

"Insanity is doing the same thing over and over again and expecting different results."

-Albert Einstein

This poignant observation by Albert Einstein reminds us of the pitfalls of complacency, particularly in our dynamic business world. In the mobility industry, traditional approaches have often followed a predictable pattern: incremental improvements on existing technologies, gradual enhancements in customer service, and a cautious attitude toward innovation. However, while these strategies have provided stability and growth, they have increasingly fallen short of meeting the demands for rapid adaptation and bold solutions.

That's what this chapter begins to unfold – a question on these traditional approaches. It's about challenging the status quo in the mobility industry and examining why a transformative shift toward future mobility is not just necessary but *inevitable*.

For decades, the mobility industry has operated within a relatively stable framework. The focus was optimizing routes, reducing costs, and enhancing service efficiency.

However, this approach ignored the broader implications: the customer experience, accessibility, environmental impact, and urban congestion, among other factors.

The traditional success metrics do not account for the increasing urgency of sustainability – or even the growing demands for inclusivity and connectivity in urban planning.

Moreover, the sector's resistance to adopting new technologies can be seen as a reluctance to change and, therefore, a potential threat to its sustainability. The digital revolution, marked by leaps in Artificial Intelligence (AI), Electric Vehicles (EVs) and Electric Vertical Takeoff and Landing (eVTOL) air transportation, autonomous driving, hyper-personalization, IoT, and big data, is reshaping customer expectations. All of that is also reshaping the possibilities in service delivery on the side. Therefore, more agile and technologically adept competitors may outpace companies that rely on outdated models.

The purpose of future mobility is beyond the mere act of moving people from point A to point B. It involves reimagining how transportation systems can enhance the quality of life, protect the environment, and create equitable opportunities for all segments of society. And that means considering Mobility-as-a-Service (MaaS) an integral component of smart cities. It will lead to smart cities where technology and data combine to offer safe, efficient, and sustainable transportation options.

However, one of the more pressing reasons to redefine the purpose of mobility is the environmental imperative. The mobility industry is a significant contributor to global carbon emissions, and the shift toward electric vehicles and renewable energy sources is both a challenge and an opportunity.

For that reason, future mobility should consider sustainability not an optional add-on but a central objective, influencing every decision from fleet management to customer engagement. Future mobility also aims to enhance connectivity in terms of network coverage and make transportation more accessible to underserved communities. That is one of the reasons why it is increasingly turning toward affordable solutions for low-income areas. Moreover, the push to design systems that accommodate individuals with disabilities is also underway. The goal is to ensure that mobility contributes to social equity and inclusion.

Rethinking Future Mobility to Drive Economic Innovation

Rethinking mobility can drive broader economic innovation. That will likely happen through a combination of catalyzed economic growth factors that boost the resilience within the industry. Not only that, but the ongoing economic innovation through future mobility can also catalyze the emergence of new industries and job opportunities — from electric vehicle manufacturing to Mobility-as-a-Service platforms, for example.

By questioning traditional business approaches and embracing the potential of future mobility, companies can align themselves with the evolving needs of society and the environment. In this chapter, we aim to critique and inspire — a call to action for forward-thinking leaders and innovators (and policymakers) to envision a future where mobility is not just a means of transportation but a founding pillar for a thriving, sustainable, and equitable world.

As we move forward, let us carry the wisdom of Einstein's words, reminding ourselves that the path to transformation requires us to think differently and act decisively.

We look at the valuable insights of challenging traditional business models in the mobility industry and passenger transportation sectors. We delve deeper into a personal journey of discovery that invites you, the leader of your enterprise, to find your own "WHY" in business. This concept, famously introduced and passionately advocated by Simon Sinek, signifies the importance – and transformative power – of understanding and articulating your core motivations.

"Finding my WHY literally changed my life. It was so powerful I wanted to share it with as many people as I could and wanted everyone I met to learn their WHY, too. It's an amazing feeling to live with purpose, on purpose."

-Simon Sinek

The Strategic Advantage of Understanding Your "WHY" in Mobility

In the passenger transportation sector, within the mobility industry, identifying your company's "WHY" goes beyond motivational speeches or mission statements—it shapes the strategic blueprint of your business. The "WHY" isn't just about purpose but about differentiating in a crowded market.

For instance, if your "WHY" revolves around sustainability, this core belief should drive innovative approaches to reducing emissions, like investing in electric fleets or integrating biofuels. That's an example of a focused initiative. This type of focus not only attracts environmentally conscious consumers but also prepares your business for future regulations to curb pollution.

Consider a company like Tesla. Its "WHY" focuses on accelerating the world's transition to sustainable energy. It's not just lofty idealism. It's a strategic stance influencing product development, marketing, and consumer engagement. Tesla's commitment to this "WHY" has led it to develop industry-leading battery technology and create a network of superchargers. As a result, it has significantly enhanced customer convenience and reduced range anxiety.

Another example is Lyft. The company started with a "WHY" centered around improving people's lives with the world's best transportation. This led to the development of the Lyft Line, which reduces user costs and the number of cars on the road, aligning with a broader vision of reducing urban congestion and environmental impact.

When your "WHY" is clear, it can directly inform how you design your services. For passenger transportation providers focused on inclusivity, this could mean ensuring that your booking omnichannel interface (Phone, Mobile App, WEB Page, Social Media, IVR, Messaging or Virtual Assistants like Alexa or Siri) is accessible to people with disabilities, different age segments or that your services cater to underserved areas, enhancing your brand's reputation and customer loyalty.

For providers driven by efficiency, the "WHY" might lead to early adoption of end-to-end software solutions to increase productivity by dramatically reducing costs and significantly increasing sales. Nowadays, complete automation is the difference between succeeding and failing – wouldn't you agree? This improves service speed and reliability to give businesses a competitive edge.

More importantly, a well-defined "WHY" can guide strategic alliances. A passenger transportation provider focusing on *Conveying Dreams Worldwide* might collaborate with open vehicle ecosystem firms to integrate their local solution to expand the service worldwide. The goal? To enhance the customer experience and safety offered to passengers.

Furthermore, companies can leverage their "WHY" to participate in policy discussions. Suppose your mission involves enhancing the mobility industry. In that case, you might advocate for infrastructure changes that support this vision, such as the development of dedicated lanes for car-sharing or the expansion of charging stations for electric vehicles.

The Social and Economic Implications of a Well-Articulated "WHY"

Customers are likelier to stay loyal to brands whose values align with theirs. In the passenger transportation sector, where choices are plentiful, a compelling "WHY" can be a decisive factor for consumers. A clear "WHY" provides a lens through which companies evaluate new technologies and innovations. It ensures that every investment or initiative is not just a pursuit of novelty but a strategic step toward realizing your core mission.

On the other hand, teams that understand and connect with their company's "WHY" are generally more engaged and productive. They see their work as part of a larger purpose. And that can be particularly motivating in industries like mobility, where the impact on the community and environment is direct and tangible. In the passenger transportation sector, your "WHY" is your guiding star; it's your strategic advantage. It informs decisions, drives innovation, and forges deeper connections with passengers and communities.

By integrating this "WHY" into every facet of the business, from operations to passenger interaction, passenger transportation providers can enhance their competitive edge and contribute to shaping the future of mobility landscapes.

The mobility industry is at a critical juncture as the world accelerates, driven by rapid technological advancements and changing consumer expectations. It faces a dual challenge: keep pace with technological innovation and adapt to increasingly sophisticated consumer demands for ease, comfort, and sustainability. To thrive, the sector must adopt disruptive thinking, move beyond incremental improvements, and pioneer substantial innovations that redefine how people move.

Today's consumer lives in a world where convenience is king. The ubiquity of smartphones has led to an expectation of services at the tap of a screen. You can order food, book vacations, buy cars, and do a thousand different activities with a single phone tap. This demand for ease and immediacy is reshaping the mobility industry, too.

Passengers no longer accept waiting in long lines, dealing with unpredictable schedules, or using cumbersome payment methods. They want seamless integration in their transportation options, synergy between different modes of transportation, and a frictionless user experience.

Where Technological Acceleration Comes In

Technological advancements are not merely improving existing systems. They are creating new possibilities that were once the realm of science fiction. Once a futuristic concept, autonomous vehicles are being tested on public roads. Electric vehicles are transitioning from niche markets to mainstream availability.

Innovations like hyperloop and air mobility (eVTOL) are exploring travel methods faster than ever.[1] These advancements are not just enhancements but are paradigm shifts in how we think about moving from one place to another.

However, these incremental changes are insufficient. The mobility industry has to adopt a disruptive mindset to stay relevant and competitive. That involves rethinking not just the technology of transportation but its very existence and relevance in individuals' lives—from how services are structured and delivered to how they are consumed and paid for.

For businesses in the mobility industry, disruptive thinking means daring to overhaul traditional models. It's all about developing and testing a system where mobility solutions are as integrated and user-friendly as smartphones. It's about anticipating changes in technology and societal norms and expectations and being at the forefront of defining those changes.

That said, entrepreneurs must foster cultures where innovation is prioritized and challenge the status quo. This might mean setting up think tanks dedicated to exploring futuristic transportation modes. Or even in startups that redefine user experience in public transit.

The future of mobility requires bold, inventive strategies that go above and beyond the conventional boundaries and

---

[1] https://fastercapital.com/topics/uncovering-the-future-of-mobility.html

preconceived notions that we are familiar with today. The world is moving toward a higher degree of convenience, efficiency, and sustainability. They are not just desirable characteristics but demanded necessities in the mobility industry.

We have also discovered that certain core principles are not just guiding but actively reshaping the industry. These principles aren't abstract notions but concrete opinions that businesses can use to realign their operations and values toward a sustainable future.

Take Tesla, for example, which is a purpose-driven business model. At its core, Tesla's mission goes beyond merely manufacturing electric vehicles. It is about revolutionizing energy consumption in transportation, too. It aims to accelerate the world's transition to sustainable energy. This commitment has driven Tesla to innovate relentlessly, pushing boundaries in battery technology and renewable energy solutions. This has made Tesla a company known for its sustainability-driven approach and products worldwide.

On the other hand, we also have user-centricity, which is pivotal to building a desirable user experience in the mobility industry. Uber's entire service model is built around enhancing user convenience and satisfaction. Many experts presume that Uber's goal is to transform urban mobility into an on-demand service that caters to its users' immediate needs.

Similarly, Amazon's principle of customer obsession teaches that understanding and anticipating customer needs isn't just good practice; it's essential for survival and growth in today's market.

Proterra, which has carved a niche in the electric transit space by designing high-performance battery solutions, also hopes to reduce greenhouse gas emissions significantly. Joby Aviation, another great example, is pioneering within the air transportation sector by developing electric vertical takeoff and landing (eVTOL) aircraft. These innovations aim to enhance mobility but in a way that aligns with pressing environmental concerns, demonstrating that operational success can go hand-in-hand with ecological objectives.

May Mobility and Waymo's approach to autonomous driving technology is another reason inclusivity matters in the industry. They have developed self-driving vehicles that cater to diverse needs, including those of individuals with disabilities. And both ensure that the future of mobility is accessible to all. This commitment reflects a broader industry shift toward designing transportation solutions – ones that are both as inclusive and innovative.

A Mobility-as-a-Service (MaaS) platform in this mix solidifies the need for integrating diverse transportation modes into a seamless, user-friendly service accessible through various channels — from mobile apps to A.I. assistants.

The principle of end-to-end business automation, as seen in companies like Zappos, can also be adapted to the mobility sector. Automating processes from booking to service delivery has significantly enhanced operational efficiency and customer satisfaction. Therefore, service features like automated scheduling, real-time vehicle tracking, streamlined payment processes, and predictive maintenance are necessary to ensure a smooth, hassle-free customer experience.

What Might a Passenger Transportation Provider in the Mobility Industry Do?

Passenger Transportation providers can harness transformative principles effectively in different ways. Tesla, for example, can integrate its core mission with every aspect of the business operation—from product design to customer interaction.

Drawing from Uber and Amazon, these leaders can also incorporate a higher degree of user experience. In this regard, continual refinement of the convenience and responsiveness of their services is critical. Similarly, Proterra and Joby Aviation show how embedding sustainable practices into service technology and operations can lead to significant short-term and long-term gains.

As a rule of thumb, provider leaders must prioritize accessibility, and the best examples include May Mobility, Waymo, Uber, and Lyft. Their goal is simple: to make mobility universal. Meanwhile, adopting a comprehensive approach to customer interaction can also make services accessible across multiple platforms.

More importantly, business leaders can automate for efficiency. Embracing automation—especially at this level of business globally—is necessary. It can streamline every aspect of operations, and the results include improved service quality, cost efficiencies, and so on.

Overall, the goal should be to prepare the organization for future demands in the mobility industry and position it as a leader in shaping a sustainable, inclusive, and efficient transportation environment.

The Role of Aligning Mobility Solutions with Human Values

During integration and widespread automation, it becomes increasingly clear that aligning mobility solutions with human values is not just beneficial – it's essential.

Human-centric values in mobility go beyond providing a service; it's about enhancing the human experience. There are initiatives like New York City's Vision Zero traffic safety project, which aims to eliminate all traffic fatalities and severe injuries while increasing safe, healthy, equitable mobility for all.[2] They also underscore how deeply transportation is intertwined with human welfare.

When we talk about aligning mobility with human values, environmental stewardship cannot be overlooked. Companies

---

[2] https://www.nyc.gov/content/visionzero/pages/

like Rivian also highlight this commitment. Rivian manufactures electric vehicles, but it is also redefining what it means to be an automotive company with a mission to keep the world adventurous forever—sustainably.[3] Their use of responsible materials and a commitment to comprehensive sustainability in vehicle production set new standards for environmental responsibility in the auto industry.

Moreover, initiatives like California's commitment to banning the sale of new gasoline cars by 2035 reflect a broader societal shift toward environmental stewardship.[4] These actions show us how powerful regulatory frameworks and business practices can be in uniting and fostering a sustainable future.

Even though most of the providers in the U.S. are still and will be using fossil fuel cars for the following years, embracing an environmental policy will help them to transition to the new mobility landscape smoothly.

Meanwhile, the principle of inclusivity in mobility solutions is also crucial. The efforts of companies like General Motors (GM) in their autonomous vehicle division – Cruise – demonstrate a forward-thinking approach to inclusivity. Cruise's self-driving cars are designed to be

---

[3] http://www.msn.com/en-us/news/technology/what-you-need-to-know-about-rivian/ar-BB1jxVgC?apiversion=v2&noservercache=1&domshim=1&renderwebcompo nents=1&wcseo=1&batchservertelemetry=1&noservertelemetry=1

[4] https://www.cnet.com/home/electric-vehicles/states-banning-new-gas-powered-cars/#:~:text=California%20is%20gearing%20up%20to,zero%20tailpipe%20e missions%20by%202035.

accessible. The aim is to provide equitable transportation solutions for all demographics, including the differently-abled or elderly.

Also, May Mobility, with their strategic partnership with Toyota,[5] shares:

"....We're building a better autonomous vehicle system that imagines every move, every millisecond. To safely move the world to a greener, more accessible future. To transform cities and solve real-world problems...."

Moreover, initiatives like Accessible Dispatch in New York City, offering wheelchair-accessible taxis, highlight the practical implementation of inclusivity in urban transportation planning. Such programs ensure that mobility solutions cater to all citizens. Moreover, it also showcases a community's commitment to social equity.

We are not talking about the future. The future is now. They operate in Ann Arbor - Michigan; Arlington – Texas; Grand Rapids – Minnesota; Miami – Florida; Phoenix – Arizona; Los Angeles, San Francisco – California; and Austin, Texas.

However, as mobility technologies advance, integrating them ethically becomes paramount. Tesla's approach to data privacy and user safety in its Autopilot and Full Self-Driving technologies also provides a benchmark for ethical considerations in new mobility tech.

---

[5] https://pressroom.toyota.com/toyota-mobility-foundation-supports-may-mobility-to-bring-autonomous-shuttle-service-to-hoosier-residents/

Then, we have federal initiatives like the U.S. Department of Transportation's guidelines for autonomous vehicles, which outline a framework for integrating these new technologies that prioritizes human safety and ethical considerations.[6]

Discovering the "Why" is essential for Passenger Transportation Providers. However, it is equally important to understand how economic models operate and the forces that shape them. This deeper comprehension enables providers to anticipate and capitalize on emerging trends, while shedding outdated concepts that have dominated the industry over the past 30 years. Embracing this dual approach—purpose-driven strategy and economic insight—empowers providers to stay competitive and adapt effectively in a rapidly evolving market.

---

[6] https://www.transportation.gov/AV

Chapter 3
Global Economic Models in the Digital Edge

"We stand on the brink of a technological revolution that will fundamentally alter the way we live, work, and relate to one another. In its scale, scope, and complexity, the transformation will be unlike anything humankind has experienced before. We do not yet know just how it will unfold, but one thing is clear: the response to it must be integrated and comprehensive, involving all stakeholders of the global polity, from the public and private sectors to academia and civil society."

- Klaus Schwab, founder and executive chairman of the World Economic Forum

As Klaus Schwab noted, we are perched on the precipice of a technological revolution that promises to redefine our lives, work, and interactions. That, too, on an unprecedented scale. This evolving scenario demands a holistic and integrated approach from all societal stakeholders, from governments and corporations to academia and civic groups.

Looking at the current economic models that govern the passenger transportation sector, we find ourselves navigating through three distinct but interconnected landscapes – the classical, digital, and post-digital frameworks. All three are outlined by Tiago Mattos, a futurist thinker, entrepreneur, and author.

Each model provides crucial insights into the industry's past, present, and future. It offers us valuable perspectives on its ongoing transformation. Starting with the classical model, we see a framework defined by physical exchange and conventional market dynamics.

Historically, this model has underscored the passenger transportation sector, emphasizing the importance of scale and efficiency. Traditional players stressed the hierarchical organizational structures and massive human resources needed to meet the transportation needs of millions. However, as we advance, the limitations of this model in addressing modern challenges such as exceptional customer experience and engagement, service availability, payment options, environmental sustainability, and urban congestion become apparent.

Transitioning into the digital era, technology can help dissolve traditional barriers and introduce a new paradigm where connectivity, data, and user experience are at the center. The rise of digital platforms like Uber and Airbnb illustrates how this model has revolutionized consumer expectations. It significantly shifted the focus from ownership to access.

These platforms have changed how services are delivered and established new market dynamics where flexibility and responsiveness are critical competitive advantages. Tesla's disruption of the automotive industry further sheds light on this digital transformation.

By integrating advanced software with electric vehicle production, Tesla has pioneered new technologies and redefined what consumers expect from their vehicles — sustainability, performance, and connectivity.

Looking beyond the digital, we enter the post-digital realm where the integration of technologies creates a seamless blend of physical and digital experiences. In this model, the focus shifts from using individual technologies to creating holistic ecosystems that enhance the efficiency and personalization of mobility solutions. The ecosystem approach encourages collaboration among stakeholders across the industry.

This includes passenger transportation providers, technology companies, regulators, urban planners, and consumers. Together, they co-create value and innovate in previously unimaginable ways. This marks a new era of possibilities for passenger transportation.

A prime example of post-digital innovation is the development of smart cities, where IoT devices, artificial intelligence, and big data converge to optimize urban mobility. Cities like Singapore and Barcelona lead the way by implementing integrated transportation systems that adapt to real-time traffic patterns, weather conditions, and urban density.[7] These systems improve the efficiency of city-wide transportation and enhance residents' quality of life by reducing congestion and pollution.

---

[7] https://www.mdpi.com/1424-8220/23/11/5206

The post-digital paradigm also emphasizes the importance of collaborative ecosystems. It encourages stakeholders across industries to unite in co-creating values beyond traditional industry boundaries.

For instance, the partnership between automotive giants and tech companies to develop autonomous vehicles is a testament to this model's potential. These collaborations are not just about sharing resources but about integrating expertise from diverse fields to innovate in ways that a single industry might not achieve alone.

The journey through classical, digital, and post-digital landscapes is not just about adopting new technologies but fundamentally rethinking how mobility can serve as a conduit for enhancing human life.

Classical Economic Models in Passenger Transportation:

In the classical economic era of passenger transportation, the sector was defined by a straightforward but rigid paradigm emphasizing ownership and physical infrastructure. During this period, transportation methods were predominantly about individuals owning personal vehicles or using public transit systems, which operated on fixed routes and schedules. This model prioritized the efficiency and reach of transportation networks, considering these the leading indicators of success.

Let's break down the critical components of this classical model:

Ownership and Use of Personal Vehicles: In the U.S., the automobile revolutionized personal mobility. Car ownership became synonymous with freedom and individual agency. This reflected a significant cultural value. The car manufacturing giants like Ford and General Motors scaled production using assembly line methods. In turn, this made vehicle ownership accessible to a broader population segment.

Public Transit Systems: These systems were designed to be comprehensive and reliable yet inflexible. Cities like New York developed extensive subway and bus systems that became integral to the city's functioning. However, the fixed routes and timetables meant that service was not always aligned with every individual's needs. As a result, it led to gaps in service efficiency.

Emergence of Livery Services: As an answer to the rigidness of public transit, livery services began to offer a more personalized form of transportation. In the U.S., these services evolved from basic taxi services to more sophisticated ride options, including limousines and private hires that catered to specific customer demands for comfort, privacy, and flexibility.

Shift Toward Service-Based Models: The classical era also planted the seeds for transitioning to service-based models. Companies like Hertz and Avis in the U.S. began offering car rentals,[8] providing people with temporary access

---

[8]https://www.reuters.com/business/autos-transportation/hertz-sell-about-20000-evs-us-fleet-2024-01-11/

to personal transportation without needing a vehicle. This model hinted at the mobility sector's potential for less ownership-focused approaches.

The classical model was effective in its time but began to show limitations as society's expectations evolved. The need for more flexible, efficient, and inclusive transportation options became apparent. As a result, this set the stage for the next evolution in economic models – digital transformation.

Transition to Digital Models: The shift to digital economic models in transportation marked a significant turning point. Introducing technology into this sector dissolved many of the rigid boundaries set by the classical models. A new type of provider emerged the TNCs (Transport Network Companies) and revolutionized the concept of mobility in the U.S. by using technology platforms to connect drivers with passengers directly. They provided flexibility that traditional public transit systems and livery services could not offer.

Uber and Lyft: These platforms boosted the digital model by emphasizing connectivity and real-time data. They made transportation on-demand, for reservation, user-centric, and highly adaptable to individual needs. Users can summon a ride with a button through apps, rate their experience, and enjoy personalized routes and schedules, paying them easily and safely.

Impact of Digitalization: The rise of these platforms showed how digital tools could leverage data to optimize routes, reduce wait times, and improve overall user satisfaction. It also highlighted the shift from owning assets (like vehicles) to facilitating services, where the value lies in the experience's quality and efficiency.

The digital model continues to evolve, pushing the boundaries of what technology can do to transform mobility. It sets the stage for the post-digital era, where the integration of various technologies will likely create even more efficient and personalized transportation solutions.

Synergy and Transformation in the Classical Economic Model

The interplay between governmental agencies and the burgeoning private sector began taking shape in the classical economic model of people transportation. Governmental entities, such as the U.S. Department of Transportation and local transit authorities, traditionally concentrated on expanding and enhancing physical infrastructure.

Their focus was on broadening the reach and capacity of public transportation systems through investments in roads, bridges, and transit networks. This approach aimed to maximize the efficiency and coverage of public transportation, which was seen as a public good essential for the functioning of society.

Meanwhile, the private sector began to carve a niche that introduced more dynamic elements into the traditional transportation landscape. This promising collaboration between public and private sectors laid the groundwork for future innovations and the gradual transition toward more integrated, technology-driven models.

Government and Private Sector Collaboration: This evolving synergy can be seen in projects like the public-private partnerships that developed around major infrastructure projects. For instance, the Denver Eagle P3 project[9] is one of U.S. transit history's largest public-private partnership endeavors. It involved significant private investment and expertise to enhance the city's commuter and light rail services. Such collaborations help share the financial burden and integrate private sector efficiency and innovation into public transportation projects.

The emergence of Private Companies Delivering Taxi and Livery Services: Within this classical framework, taxi and livery services began to provide an alternative to the rigidness of public transit systems. Companies like Yellow Cab, black Car, and limo services in the U.S. offered more flexible services than bus or train schedules. This allowed for door-to-door service and responding more directly to individual consumer needs. These services began to hint at a market-driven approach to passenger transportation, prioritizing consumer convenience and adaptability.

---

[9] https://www.transportation.gov/buildamerica/projects/project-highlights/eagle-p3-project-denver-co

The Significant Move Toward Service-Oriented Models

The role of livery and private passenger transportation companies marked a clear shift from traditional, infrastructure-focused transportation models toward service-oriented and customer-centric models. This shift was characterized by a move away from the structures of fixed schedules and routes dictated by public transportation systems – and the isolation of personal vehicle ownership.

The private sector started to leverage technology to increase operational agility. For instance, the advent of GPS and mobile technology allowed these services to optimize routing, reduce wait times, and improve service reliability, directly benefiting the customer experience. Additionally, rental and leasing models, like those pioneered by Enterprise Rent-A-Car, provided consumers with temporary, flexible access to personal transportation without the long-term financial commitment of ownership. Then began the era where service diversity reached new heights.

This era saw the expansion and introduction of various sub-niches within the passenger transportation sector. Shuttle services, microtransit, NEMET (Non-Emergency Medical Transportation), and livery (luxury black car/limousine) services catered to specific market segments to provide tailored transportation solutions that addressed unique consumer needs.

As these private entities grew, they increasingly incorporated technology for route optimization and service booking, payment, and customer feedback. This responsiveness to consumer preferences pushed us toward a new era of mobility where passenger experience was more important than before.

While the classical economic model laid the foundational frameworks of mobility through extensive infrastructure development, the innovative approaches of livery services and private companies truly transformed the passenger transportation sector. By prioritizing passenger experience and operational agility and exploring novel business models, these entities moved beyond the limitations of traditional public transportation systems.

They introduced dynamism and flexibility previously unseen in the sector, signaling a shift toward a more holistic approach emphasizing service diversity, technological integration, and consumer-centric solutions.

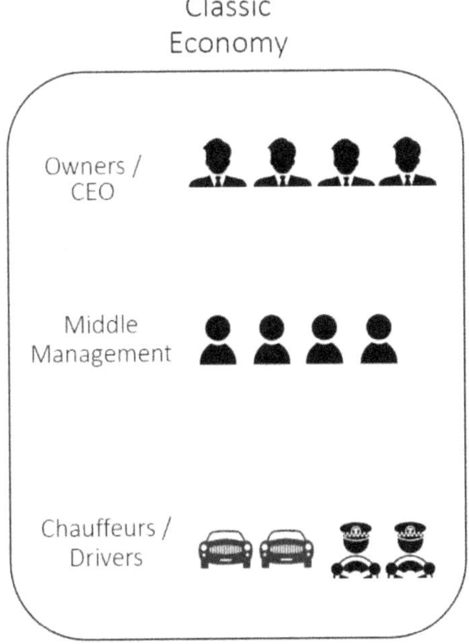

Digital Economic Model in Passenger Transportation

The rise of the digital economy profoundly affected various industries, with passenger transportation experiencing one of the most significant overhauls. This shift was catalyzed by the advent of Transportation Network Companies (TNCs) like Uber and Lyft, which have revolutionized how we access and use transportation through the power of digital platforms.

TNCs represent a major development in the passenger transportation sector by introducing a model that blends technology with the traditional ride-sharing service. They disrupt the old taxi and livery services by implementing a peer-to-peer framework that uses sophisticated algorithms to match drivers with passengers efficiently. This digital matchmaking is done in real time, a significant leap from traditional public transport's pre-scheduled, route-bound operations or the solitary nature of personal vehicle ownership.

One of the standout features of the digital economic model is its focus on personalization. TNCs utilize vast amounts of user data to enhance operational efficiency and user satisfaction, like ride tracking, estimated arrival time, and fare estimates, all tailored to the individual's current needs and preferences.

Furthermore, these platforms continually adapt and refine user experiences based on feedback and behavioral data. This ensures each user's experience is as convenient and pleasant as possible. For instance, consider how TNCs adapts its service with options like pool riding and charters, which offers shared rides at a lower cost.

Black Vehicles and SUVs may be available for users looking for a more premium service. This flexibility caters to a broad range of preferences and needs and enhances user engagement by providing choices that align with different customer segments.

Attention-Driven and Freemium Models

The digital economic model also innovates in its engagement and revenue generation approach. Using attention-driven strategies, TNCs engage users by offering real-time solutions and personalized services. Waze, a GPS navigation software, provides driving directions based on real-time traffic conditions. All of that is possible through user-generated updates.

This model extends user engagement beyond mere functionality to create a dynamic, interactive platform where users contribute to and benefit from the shared information. Moreover, the freemium model employed by many digital platforms plays a crucial role in expanding the user base. By offering basic services for free while charging for premium features, TNCs make their services accessible to a larger audience while creating avenues for enhanced revenue through upgraded offerings.

Beyond individual service enhancements, TNCs influence a broader digital and physical ecosystem. They act as hubs that connect various aspects of people's daily lives, from commuting and logistics to how cities are planned and managed. Integrating these services into the broader urban infrastructure is instrumental in fostering more connected, efficient cities.

Take Uber's partnerships with local businesses and events, for example. It is to provide a seamless transportation experience that supports mobility, local economies, and community engagement. These partnerships demonstrate how TNCs are integral to the broader digital economy. They affect how urban environments and economies function.

For now, the digital economic model is set to evolve significantly. It promises to bring further innovations that will redefine the very fabric of the mobility industry. With AI and machine learning advancements, the potential for even more personalized, efficient, and integrated transportation solutions is on the horizon.

In the Digital Economic Model, TNCs and process automation are as important as the ecosystem to achieve exponential growth within a high-concentration and controlled environment.

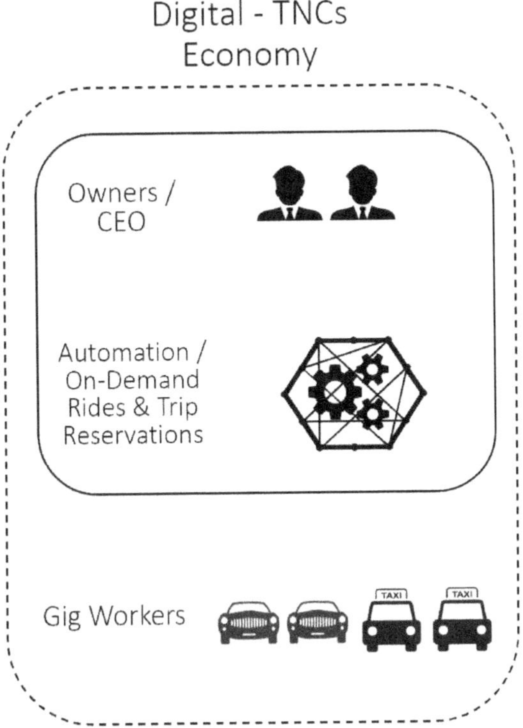

The Post-Digital Economic Model in Passenger Transportation:

In the post-digital era, the landscape of people transportation is undergoing a profound transformation. This new phase extends beyond the initial digital disruptions caused by TNCs. This model indicates a step toward a realm where technology integrates unconventionally to reach new heights of sophistication and integration.

The post-digital economic model uses advancements in artificial intelligence (AI), blockchain, and the Internet of

Things (IoT) to create (and sustain) a holistic, ecosystem-centric approach to transportation.

Transportation Network Companies (TNCs) are at the vanguard of this evolution. They employ digital-first strategies to incorporate emerging technologies that enhance operational efficiencies and user experiences.

AI technologies refine operational aspects such as dynamic route optimization and intelligent matching algorithms. These technologies enable TNCs to pair passengers with drivers more efficiently, reducing wait times and optimizing journey durations.

For example, Uber uses machine learning algorithms to predict rider demand, which helps position drivers in areas most likely needed before the demand spikes. On the other hand, blockchain technology is being explored for its potential to bring unparalleled transparency and security to transactions within the TNCs ecosystem. It can provide a verifiable and secure framework that builds trust among users and service providers.

IoT technology facilitates a more interconnected transportation environment, yet another technological advancement. Vehicles equipped with IoT devices can communicate with traffic systems, other vehicles, and infrastructure to create a mesh of data that can dramatically enhance the efficiency and safety of travel.

For instance, smart traffic lights can adjust signal timings based on real-time traffic flow data from connected vehicles.

It can also reduce congestion and improve road safety. As TNCs evolve, their focus shifts from providing ride-sharing services to becoming integral parts of comprehensive Mobility-as-a-Service (MaaS) ecosystems.

This model aims to offer users access to various transportation options through a unified platform that seamlessly integrates public transit, ride-share, bike-share, and other modes of transport. This approach simplifies user interaction with multiple transportation services and enhances the efficiency of urban mobility systems.

Integrating scooter rental services into existing apps allows users to choose between a car ride or an electric scooter rental from the same app based on their preference, trip distance, and traffic conditions. This type of integration represents a shift toward more adaptive, user-centered mobility solutions that cater to the varied needs of urban commuters.

However, in the post-digital era, TNCs are also increasingly focused on their operations' environmental and social implications. For example, more TNCs are incorporating electric and hybrid vehicles into their fleets. Take Lyft, which aims to achieve a 100% electric or zero-emission fleet by 2030.[10] Such initiatives reflect a growing commitment to reducing the environmental footprint of mobility services.

---

[10] https://www.lyft.com/blog/posts/inside-lyfts-quest-to-get-drivers-to-adoptevs#:~:text=In%20June%202020%2C%20Lyft%20announced,of%20all%20new%20vehicles%20sold.

Another critical focus area is ensuring that transportation services are accessible to all, including those with disabilities. To address that, TNCs are implementing features like vehicle modifications for wheelchair access and developing apps that are more accessible to users with visual and hearing impairments.[11]

The post-digital economic model represents a significant evolution in the passenger transportation sector. It highlights the importance of technology integration, ecosystem connectivity, environmental responsibility, and social inclusivity. These trends promise to reshape how we travel and connect within our cities to craft a more sustainable and inclusive future for the mobility industry.

In the post-digital economic model, TNCs and process automation are less important than the ecosystem in achieving hyper growth within a connected and decentralized environment.

The Rise of New Success Metrics in the Post-Digital Era

In the post-digital era, the evaluation of success for TNCs and broader transportation services has shifted dramatically. Traditional metrics centered primarily on financial gains have given way to a more holistic set of criteria emphasizing environmental sustainability, customer satisfaction, and social impact. This evolution reflects a more profound

---

[11] https://www.sfmta.com/sites/default/files/reports-and-documents/2019/05/tnc_and_disable_access_whit_paper-rev11_2.pdf

societal shift toward valuing businesses for their economic contributions and broader global influence.

As we've witnessed, environmental impact is a critical success metric in today's passenger transportation sector. Companies are increasingly held accountable for their carbon footprint and are expected to implement practices that mitigate environmental harm.

Uber's Green Plan will become a fully electric, zero-emission platform by 2040.[12] This goal aligns with broader environmental objectives and enhances the company's brand as a responsible corporate citizen. Furthermore, modern transportation services are also measured by how well they meet passenger expectations for convenience, safety, and reliability.

Using technology to enhance user experiences—such as app-based controls, real-time tracking, and AI-driven support systems—is now standard. The success of these initiatives is often captured through detailed customer feedback mechanisms, allowing companies to adjust their services to fit user needs.

There is a growing emphasis on passenger transportation services' inclusivity. Success for contemporary TNCs involves ensuring that mobility solutions are accessible to all

---

[12] https://www.reuters.com/article/world/asia-pacific/uber-promises-100-electric-vehicles-by-2040-commits-800-million-to-help-drive-idUSKBN25Z2I1/

segments of society, including underserved communities and individuals with disabilities.

The expanded role of TNCs in the post-digital era positions them as pivotal elements within an interconnected mobility network. These companies are not just service providers but critical players in a larger ecosystem that includes public transportation, private vehicles, biking, and walking options.

It's worth mentioning that many TNCs are now partnering between them and with city transit systems to fill gaps in service. The goal is to offer "last-mile" microtransit solutions that help users connect from transit stops to their final destinations.

Uber Transit in Denver integrates real-time public transit data into the Uber app, allowing users to easily combine transit and ride-share options in a single journey. The focus has shifted toward facilitating travel experiences that are not only seamless but also sustainable. This involves optimizing routes to reduce travel times and emissions, using data analytics to predict and manage demand, and incorporating sustainable practices in every aspect of operation.

Exploring further, TNCs are central to creating a mobility ecosystem that prioritizes user convenience and sustainability. This system is designed to be flexible. This is because it allows users to choose the best mode of transportation for their needs at any given time and, for that reason, makes mobility more adaptive and efficient.

Is There a New Vision for Mobility?

In the post-digital economy, the mobility ecosystem's significance surpasses the individual roles of TNCs. It embodies a vision where transportation is about reaching a destination and enhancing the quality of life, protecting the environment, and fostering a more inclusive society.

The model continues to evolve; it promises to further revolutionize our concepts of mobility, connectivity, and urban living, positioning TNCs as transportation facilitators and architects of a more connected and sustainable future.

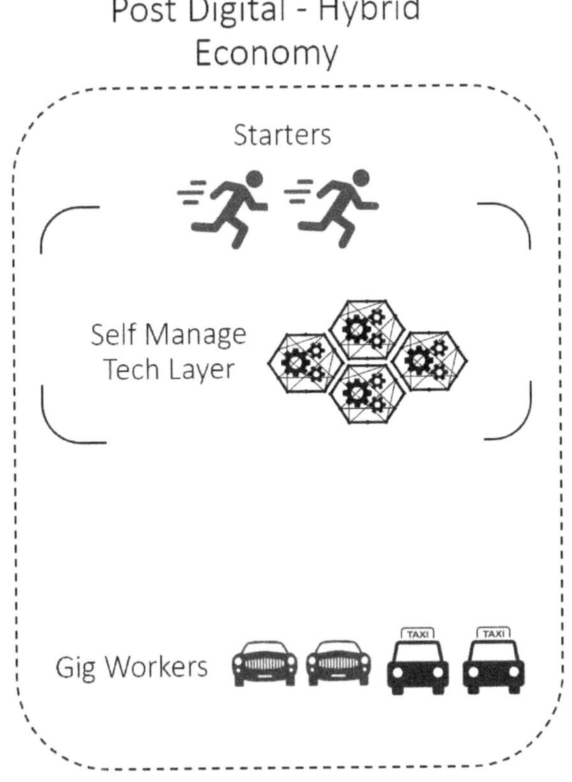

The future of mobility in the post-digital era is characterized by a holistic approach where technology, environmental consciousness, and social inclusivity converge to redefine the essence of passenger transportation. This future is not merely about technological advancements but creating a sustainable framework where mobility solutions contribute positively to society and the environment.

As we look ahead, AI, IoT, and blockchain integration will become more refined. It will most likely lead to smarter mobility solutions that are highly responsive to user needs and environmental impacts. Cities could see a more synchronized mobility network that smartly manages traffic flows, reduces congestion, and minimizes emissions through intelligent transportation systems.

The concept of MaaS is expected to expand. It will offer more comprehensive services that cover various modes of transportation through a single access point. This expansion will likely include an increased use of autonomous vehicles. Subsequently, this will blur the lines between different transportation modes and create a seamless travel experience. In addition, future mobility models will empower consumers like never before.

They will offer unprecedented control over travel choices. Enhanced data analytics and more user-friendly interfaces will allow individuals to optimize their transportation based on cost, time, comfort, or environmental impact. Against the backdrop of this evolution, there will be an evolution in the robust for robust regulatory and ethical frameworks that will ensure that advancements in mobility are safe, equitable, and beneficial for all.

It will most prominently include addressing concerns related to data privacy, cybersecurity, and the ethical implications of autonomous and AI-driven systems. The successful realization of this vision will require concerted efforts from all stakeholders – governments, private companies, non-profits, and communities. Collaborative efforts will be crucial in addressing the challenges and harnessing the opportunities that arise from this rapidly evolving industry.

The new post-digital economy model is a pivotal moment for the mobility industry. The tide of technology, an abundant mindset, and provider organization transformations will level up all stakeholders.

As we will learn in the following chapters, in this new economy model and with advanced technology as a catalyzer, all mobility providers will be able to compete with the TNCs' goliaths of the market. The post-digital economy's impact on the world will be one thousand times bigger than the impact on humanity of the Industrial Revolution.

In this new economic model, **entrepreneurs and government agencies with ambition and an abundance mindset** will thrive and rapidly scale their operations at a hyper-exponential pace.

The next chapter will dive deeper into how the transition to this new economic model will empower all stakeholders in the mobility industry, unlocking unprecedented opportunities for growth and innovation.

Chapter 4
Mastering the Shift in Economic Models

"To improve is to change; to be perfect is to change often."

-Winston Churchill

The mobility industry was once dominated by static routing and vehicle ownership models. But today, it is characterized by fluid, technology-driven dynamics that require crucial market players to be adaptive. Recently, new monetization models emerged to transform the delivery and consumption of mobility services in the passenger transportation sector.

This chapter expects to investigate these changes and their crucial driving factors. We will also discuss the difficulties and the new opportunities they present.

Strategic Adaptation to New Economic Realities

A thorough comprehension of the forces at play and the resources available to effectively navigate them is necessary to adapt to the new economic realities. Organizations and policymakers should consider how the mix of artificial intelligence, IoT, autonomous technology, communications, and electromobility is upgrading functional efficiencies. They must also consider the impact of their integration on the overall market designs and consumer assumptions.

Furthermore, key players must understand consumer behavior and expectations to remain competitive, especially in an environment with changing consumer preferences. It's safe to say that there is a significant shift toward more personalized, on-demand transportation services and the rising consumer emphasis on sustainability.

Just as economic models change, so do the regulatory environments in which they operate. The questions revolve around how states and global bodies answer the difficulties presented by new advancements and action plans. There must be strategies surrounding emerging security concerns, network protection, and the requirement for new structures to oversee independent and shared vehicle ecosystems.

The evolution from classical to post-classical economic models signifies a pivotal shift in the locus of power within the passenger transportation sector. Traditionally, power structures in economic models were top-heavy, characterized by centralized decision-making and resource control.

This setup restricted the ability of individuals and local communities to influence or partake in shaping the services they use daily. However, as we transition into the post-classical era, these dynamics are undergoing radical changes, increasingly favoring a model prioritizing empowerment and decentralized control.

Digital services and online platforms offer users and transportation service providers more control. It shows the industry's shift toward decentralization in the transportation sector. By giving consumers unprecedented control over their mobility options, ridesharing apps, for instance, have revolutionized how power is distributed within the passenger transportation sector.

The operational aspects of these services can now be directly influenced by passengers choosing their preferred rides, selecting routes, and providing real-time feedback. This shift significantly enhances user satisfaction and engagement. Hence, it also makes transportation a service and a tailored experience that respects individual preferences.

This empowerment is built on technology, which enables consumers and communities to have greater influence and participation. Implementing cutting-edge innovations empowers more customized and responsive administrations.

Smartphone Apps for public transportation, for instance, incorporate real-time data that allows users to optimize their routes, avoid delays, and make plans on the go. In turn, it effectively puts them in control of their commutes.

Furthermore, the same level of empowerment also extends to the community level, where collective input and collaborative decision-making are becoming influential in the transportation planning and implementation processes. For example, Drives and local area-driven travel advancement programs show this pattern.

Public travel experts in urban areas like Portland and San Francisco frequently discuss individual needs for public transportation with the nearby local area. This leads to innovative arrangements and creates a more progressive and socially cohesive methodology for public transportation planning.

Understanding and catering to the empowered consumer is essential for creating value in today's market. For passenger transportation providers, this implies creating proficient and inventive administrations adaptable and receptive to individual necessities.

Pivotal Roles of Transparency and Inclusivity in Business Practices

Inclusion and transparency are now essential aspects of business operations. Consumers and local area partners progressively expect transparency about how items are made, who makes them, and these cycles' natural and social effects.

As a result, TNCs have made significant efforts to increase transparency regarding their rates, drivers' ratings, environmental impact and safety measures. This includes in-depth reporting on safety incidents and efforts to cut carbon emissions, which helps to build trust and improve their brand's reputation.

In the post-old-style period, effective organizations also perceived the significance of contributing emphatically to the networks they serve. This includes something other than financial commitments. It could support a reasonable metropolitan turn of events. All of that further develops availability, and it is evenhanded to guarantee that administrations are available.

In cities like San Francisco, for instance, shared bicycle programs give visitors and residents a cheap way to get around and help reduce pollution and traffic congestion. That allows the community to achieve its larger environmental goals.

These movements significantly impact the mobility industry because of their central role in daily life and critical ecological impact. The sector's shift from rigid, traditional service models toward more user-driven and flexible options reflects a broader trend toward democratizing the conception and delivery of services.

Organizations are currently investigating models that focus on consumer contribution in help customization, for example, secluded vehicles that can be adjusted for various purposes or vehicle sharing stages that coordinate passenger inclinations into vehicle designation calculations. This shift influences existing plans of action and offers new opportunities for advancement and development that align with the requirements of an increasingly aware society.

The passenger transportation sector's future will probably be characterized by how well it can adjust to the new and evolving standards of strength, inclusivity, and supportability. Thus, it will fulfill the present consumers' advancing needs and form more robust and more energetic networks.

Consider how technology is being used to empower citizens in cities like Boston and Seattle. Seattle's "One

Center City" drive includes multi-office coordination that uses public input to streamline metropolitan portability and make a more incorporated transportation organization.[13] In Boston, the "Go Boston 2030" vision advances local area commitment to arranging future transportation organizations, underlining openness and maintainability.[14]

These instances point to a broader trend toward systems that are not only innovative and effective but also inclusive and accommodating of the requirements of all users. The passenger transportation sector is setting an example for other industries by adopting a more distributed model of empowering all the involved stakeholders (Consumers, Drivers, Providers and Communities) rather than the traditional hierarchical model.

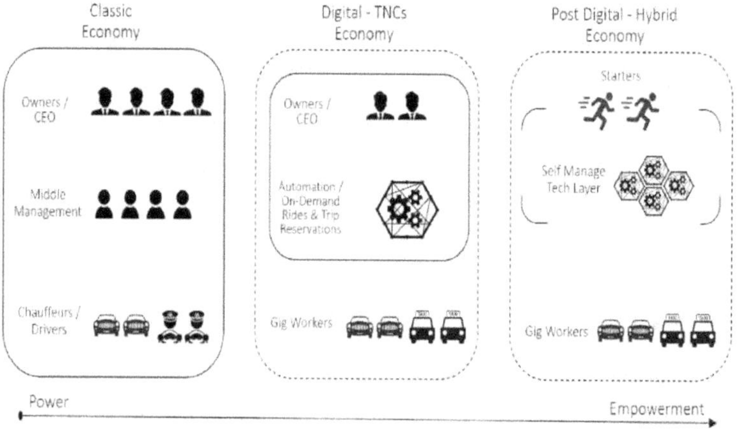

---

[13]https://www.seattle.gov/Documents/Departments/SDOT/About/Documen tLibrary/SeattlePedestrianMasterPlan.pdf

[14]https://assets.ctfassets.net/1hf11j69ure4/B6NLxlOVxTVMNbHEvFaQE/ 700f4762bae9290f91327a7e01e2f09/Boston-Green-New-Deal-August-2020-FINAL.pdf

The Move from Scarcity to Abundance

The shift from scarcity to abundance is a topic of interest in economic models. It represents a significant change in mindset and operational strategies across various industries, particularly mobility. This shift is generally driven by headway in innovation and changes in consumer conduct. Why? To create distance from the conventional spotlight on restricted assets to a unique methodology that expands existing resources.

In traditional models, vehicles and infrastructure were regarded as scarce commodities. Moreover, their use was determined by ownership and limited accessibility. Now, the digital revolution has fundamentally altered this perception, as demonstrated by the rise of the sharing economy. TNCs and city-wide bike-sharing programs demonstrate that existing resources can be effectively utilized to significantly increase utility and accessibility without requiring proportionate increases in physical assets.

For instance, car-sharing platforms use technology to enable many people to utilize a single vehicle according to their scheduling requirements, significantly increasing the vehicle's utility and effectiveness. Similarly, bike-sharing programs use technologies like station-free parking and digital tracking to enable bikes to serve many users daily in urban areas, thereby reducing emissions and easing traffic congestion.

Mechanical developments have also been vital in changing monetary shortage into overflow. GPS innovation, versatile networks, and information examination are only a few instances of how tech has re-imagined what is conceivable in transportation.

These advancements have empowered constant following and proficient steering, which has amplified the utilization of transportation resources. GPS technology, for instance, enables logistics companies like FedEx and UPS to optimize delivery routes. It has resulted in annual fuel savings of millions of gallons and significant cost savings for operations.

By analyzing usage patterns and trends, Passenger Transportation providers can better predict demand, allocate resources more effectively, and improve service availability and passenger satisfaction.

For example, New York City's Metropolitan Transportation Authority utilizes enormous amounts of information to break down traveler streams and upgrade administration plans.

Meanwhile, the transition from scarcity to abundance significantly impacts passenger transportation's environmental sustainability. It amplifies the utilization of shared vehicles and public travel arrangements, and computerized stages assist with diminishing the number of vehicles out and about, lowering discharges, and reducing the metropolitan space expected for leaving.

More importantly, organizations like Zipcar have added electric vehicles (EVs) to their fleet. They offer clients the advantages of EV innovation without requiring individual possession.

A study confirms the prospect of utilizing electric vehicles within the growing and environment-conscious mobility market with a broader range of user options.[15] This facilitates the public's familiarization with electric vehicle technology and makes sustainable transportation more accessible.[16]

At long last, this time of overflow engages buyers by giving more decisions and better administrations. It also empowers networks to outfit aggregate assets for more noteworthy public advantage, like better metropolitan preparation and diminished ecological impression.

However, it also requires digital tools to gather feedback and tailor solutions to specific local requirements. Urban areas like Portland and San Francisco increasingly involve local communities in transportation planning. To create transportation systems that are both more efficient and long-lasting, this collaborative strategy makes use of the vast amount of information and preferences held by the community.

The shift from a scarcity mindset to one of abundance is also indicated by the rise in the adoption of electric vehicles (EVs), mainly when using renewable energy sources in transportation. This development is upheld by critical

---

[15] https://www.eea.europa.eu/en/topics/in-depth/electric-vehicles
[16] https://www.sciencedirect.com/science/article/pii/S0038012122003123

headways in battery innovation, which have worked on productivity and brought down the expenses of EVs, making them a reasonable choice for a more extensive section of the populace.

Take, for instance, Tesla's impact on the US electric vehicle market.[17] Tesla has progressed battery innovation and extended the charging framework, which has been essential in advancing the reception of electric vehicles. One of the primary concerns potential users have regarding the range of electric vehicles is addressed by the company's initiative to establish a nationwide network of Superchargers, which ensures that EV owners can easily travel long distances.

The strategic use of big data and analytics, on the other hand, transforms transportation systems and makes them smarter and more responsive to user needs. Data-driven solutions enable precise traffic management, efficient routing, and accurate demand forecasting. This optimization results in better resource allocation, enhanced service delivery, and improved overall user experiences.

For instance, cities like Los Angeles utilize data from various sensors and traffic cameras to manage traffic flow more effectively.[18] Integrating this data into dynamic

---

[17] https://www.iea.org/reports/global-ev-outlook-2024/trends-in-the-electric-vehicle-industry#:~:text=In%20the%20United%20States%2C%20Tesla,2020%20to%2045%25%20in%202023.

[18] https://www.sciencedirect.com/science/article/pii/S2666691X24000277

signaling systems allows the city to adjust traffic lights in real time to reduce congestion and enhance road safety.

Additionally, the shift toward an abundance-based economic model emphasizes the significance of collaboration across the transportation ecosystem. Communities, businesses, and government agencies can collaborate to solve complex problems and use collective resources to encourage innovation.

The Smart City Challenge, an initiative launched by the U.S. Department of Transportation, is a prime example of this collaborative approach. The department released the program to encourage the development and implementation of innovative public transportation solutions.[19]

Using advanced technology, data, and creative intelligence, cities were expected to propose transportation ideas that would promote sustainability, reduce traffic congestion, and improve safety – among other public transportation goals. Columbus, Ohio, won the challenge in 2016, earning the $50m grant prize to implement its proposed solutions.[20]

Integrating Solutions Across the Value Chain

Solutions that span the entire value chain Integration in the whole value chain is necessary for the mobility industry

---

[19]https://www.transportation.gov/sites/dot.gov/files/docs/Smart%20City%20O%20Challenge%20Lessons%20Learned.pdf

[20] https://www.forbes.com/sites/tiriasresearch/2016/06/24/columbus-wins-the-smart-city-challenge-and-50m-in-grants/

to establish a sustainable ecosystem. This all-encompassing methodology includes vehicle makers, specialist co-ops, framework designers, and administrative bodies.

It boosts individual businesses' competitiveness and contributes to broader objectives like accessibility, efficiency, and environmental responsibility. For instance, for new technologies to be effectively supported and incorporated into the existing infrastructure, electric vehicles (EVs) must be developed by battery manufacturers, automobile manufacturers, energy providers, and government agencies.

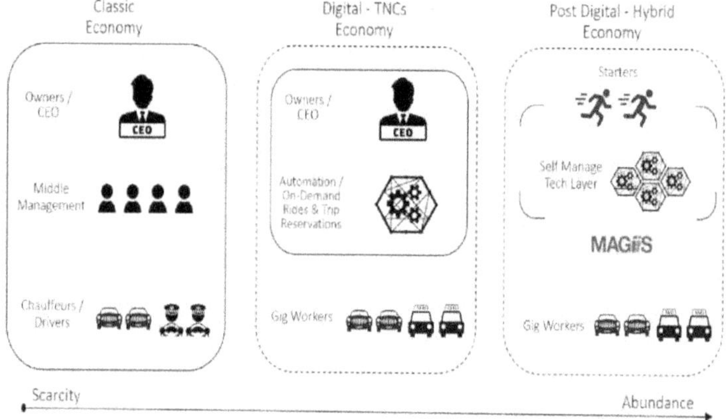

The passenger transportation sector has fundamentally changed due to economic models' shift from scarcity to abundance. This shift advocates for a future where technology, collaboration, and sustainable practices create an abundant mobility ecosystem with opportunities for growth and innovation. What's more important is that it challenges the conventional notions of competition and resource limitations. For now, the future of transportation looks promising, with greater inclusivity, sustainability, and efficiency, as we continue to investigate and embrace these changes.

Implications for the Future – The Course of Passenger Transportation

The passenger transportation sector is on the verge of a transformative era as it negotiates the shifting economic models — from classical to digital and post-digital — that are currently in use.

This change involves more than just adopting new technologies. It also involves redefining mobility to meet the needs of today's consumers, technological advancements, and society.

The changing consumer assumptions drive the transportation area to zero in addition to adaptability, ecological effect, and customized encounters. These expectations are increasingly met by technological advancements that enable smarter and more connected services.

For instance, coordinating augmented reality (AR) into route frameworks can give clients a more intelligent and spontaneous way to explore complex city conditions. Apps like Google Maps are beginning to use augmented reality (AR) to improve real-time directions.

The process involves overlaying virtual path markers on the live camera feed, where apps like Google Maps make navigation more engaging and clearer. This is especially engaging and helpful for younger users or people unfamiliar with the area.

As cultural mindfulness regarding manageability heightens, the passenger transportation sector also addresses such concerns by coordinating more eco-accommodating practices.

That includes using electric buses in public transit fleets. In fact, by 2030, cities like Los Angeles hope to have all their bus fleets run on electric power. This change helps lessen the carbon impression of public travel and sets a norm for different urban areas to follow. As a result, it advances toward a more extensive development and economical metropolitan versatility.

In addition, universal accessibility to transportation is becoming increasingly important. This means making it easier for people with disabilities to get around physically. Moreover, it also involves developments that ensure underserved groups can afford mobility solutions. Projects like San Francisco's Muni Available Administrations Program show us how transportation frameworks are developing to address these issues and guarantee that everybody has equivalent admittance to versatility choices.

Advancements in AI and IoT are also set to further transform the mobility industry by making systems more intelligent and interconnected. AI-driven predictive maintenance can dramatically increase the efficiency and lifespan of transportation infrastructure by forecasting needs and automating care.

IoT, on the other hand, facilitates real-time data sharing between vehicles and infrastructure, enhancing the safety and efficiency of transportation networks. For instance, smart traffic management systems that use AI and IoT to adjust signal timings based on real-time traffic data can reduce congestion and minimize waiting times at intersections.

As we conclude our exploration of the evolving economic models within the mobility industry, it's clear that traditional paradigms no longer suffice. The rapid pace of technological advancements, shifting consumer expectations, and the drive toward more sustainable and inclusive practices are reshaping how we define and deliver mobility services. This new economic reality challenges established norms and calls for bold, transformative thinking.

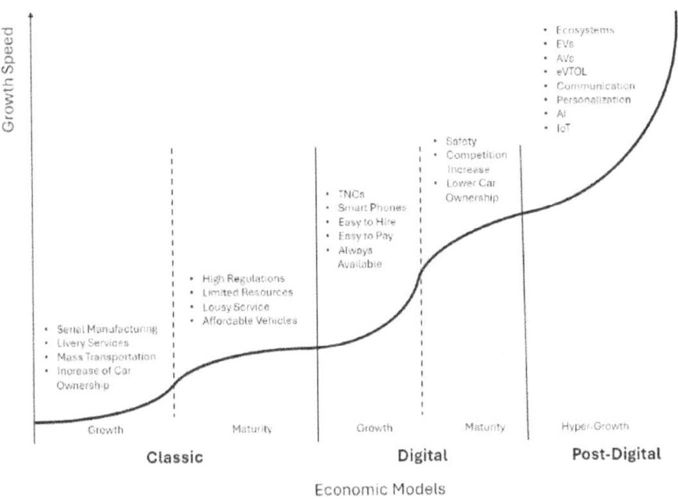

Adapting to these changes is not just about survival; it's about thriving. Organizations that embrace strategic adaptation, harness cutting-edge technologies, and respond to the empowered consumer's needs are poised to lead this transformation. The shift from scarcity to abundance, the decentralization of power, and the reimagining of consumer-driven experiences highlight the need for a new mindset prioritizing collaboration, inclusivity, and technological innovation.

The next chapter will explore how to thrive within a connected mobility ecosystem. We'll uncover practical insights and strategies tailored for ridesharing, livery services, and passenger transportation fleets as they navigate this complex, technology-driven landscape. By understanding and embracing the forces at play, mobility providers can position themselves as participants and leaders in the future of transportation.

Chapter 5
How to Thrive in a Connected Mobility Ecosystem: Key Insights for Ridesharing, Livery, and Passenger Transportation Fleets

"Not everything that is faced can be changed. But nothing can be changed until it is faced."

-James Baldwin

This chapter investigates the particular ramifications for people transportation providers, attire tasks, and more extensive transportation fleets (Ridesharing, livery, microtransit, paratransit, Non-Emergency Medical Transportation (NEMET), and others). The emphasis is on how these services can flourish in a sector progressively characterized by coordination, innovation, and evolving customer assumptions.

Technological Disruption as a Catalyst for Transformation

Companies like Tesla, Lucid Motors, BYD, and Rivian are active participants in the rapidly evolving field of automotive technology. They are trailblazers shaping the future. These organizations are acclimating to industry drifts and are making them, generally adjusting what customers anticipate from their vehicles and setting new principles for execution and supportability.

Tesla's strategy has fundamentally altered the automotive landscape. Tesla has rethought the role that the automobile plays in our lives, and it's not just about replacing gas engines with electric ones. High-capacity batteries, advanced autonomous driving features, and integrated renewable energy solutions make Tesla automobiles more than just vehicles. They have become part of a larger eco-friendly lifestyle.

The new proposal for the RoboTaxi service is expected to reshape the mobility industry and challenge service providers, including governments and vehicle manufacturers. As a direct business-to-consumer model (B2C), it can influence existing transportation providers available to the public while adding pressure on policymakers to adopt responsive regulatory frameworks. The new policies will consider autonomous vehicles operating in the passenger transportation sector while ensuring passenger safety and commuting rights. Thus, new opportunities will emerge for new providers with this significant development.

On the other hand, Lucid Motors is redefining what luxury means in an electric vehicle. The Lucid Air, known for its impressive battery range and plush interiors, challenges existing luxury electric vehicles. It proves that environmental friendliness does not necessarily need to sacrifice comfort or performance.

Lucid's vehicles are equipped with advanced drivetrains that rival and sometimes surpass traditional high-performance luxury cars in speed and handling. As a result, they appeal to a demographic that prizes innovation and elegance.

Passenger transportation providers, especially ridesharing, livery, and microtransit services, are set to be significantly influenced by innovations from companies like Tesla and Lucid. Beyond meeting corporate responsibility goals, these providers are transitioning to electric vehicles (EVs) in response to improving EV affordability, increasing consumer demand for environmentally friendly options, and the desire for cost-effective transportation without compromising quality.

These insights are helpful to both new and established passenger transportation providers. They stress the significance of saddling state-of-the-art innovation, zeroing in on supportability, and adjusting consumer assumptions to stay serious. Organizations that mirror these trailblazers' versatility and groundbreaking strategies are strategically situated to lead in the new passenger transportation period.

Moreover, the development of extensive charging networks by companies like Tesla, which has established a widespread Supercharger network, is mitigating one of the major hurdles to EV adoption for fleet operators—the availability of rapid charging options. Tesla's opening of its Supercharger network to other vehicles in 2023 is a game changer fostering the Abundance mindset in the mobility industry.

The Shift Toward Consumer-Centric Focus in the Mobility Industry

TNCs, forerunners of a new era in passenger transportation, have revolutionized passenger transportation. These businesses have transformed mobility by making each ride a customizable and convenient experience by placing their customers' preferences at the center of their strategies. This goes beyond merely making adjustments to the options that are already available.

Transportation Network Companies (TNCs) are redefining mobility in unique ways, but they all share a common approach—placing customer preferences at the center of their operations. This shift is transforming passenger transportation, bringing new comfort levels, flexibility, and choice. As a result, it is reshaping how metropolitan residents travel from one place to another.

They have also made the booking process extremely user-friendly by utilizing technology to transform it. With just a few taps, consumers can book a ride, track the driver's location in real-time, and choose from various vehicles and services to meet their specific requirements – for example, using a shared, budget-friendly ride or a private, **Luxurious** option. This consistent methodology has helped their passengers and laid out another norm for passenger assistance in transportation.

Furthermore, creating some distance from the unbending designs of conventional taxi and livery providers, TNCs make a range of decisions that take special care of different passenger needs and spending plan limitations. Because of this adaptability, the services can provide a customized transportation experience that public transportation systems cannot match, regardless of whether a passenger is looking for a low-cost ride-sharing option or a more expensive option for a solo or **Luxury Trip**.

The TNCs' new business model excels in customer support because their apps provide support around the clock. This instant communication facilitates a constantly evolving service platform to prioritize user satisfaction and safety. It allows the passengers to report any concerns they may have during their journey.

It also accounts for easy-to-hire, always-available, frictionless payments consumers demand regarding transparent rates. In essence, both businesses set convenience and passenger service as top priorities. Traditional taxi services and other transportation providers have been forced to rethink how they interact with passengers and provide services due to TNCs' success. Their imaginative practices have provoked a flood of upgrades. These most prominently include redesigned computerized frameworks, improved client correspondence channels, and a more extensive scope of transportation choices to satisfy the changing needs of consumers.

Strategic Insights for Passenger Transportation Management and Ridesharing Services

The passenger-first models championed by TNCs also provide critical lessons for others in the passenger transportation ecosystem. They are particularly helpful in managing large fleets for ridesharing and similar passenger transportation services.

For instance, investing in advanced technology to elevate the passenger experience is crucial. This might involve adopting intuitive omnichannel booking systems, diversifying vehicle options, or employing sophisticated data analytics to efficiently anticipate and meet consumer demands. In response to growing environmental consciousness among consumers, passenger transportation providers are increasingly incorporating electric vehicles and promoting personalized rides.

Moreover, traditional transportation providers increasingly collaborate with technology firms to harness their expertise and integrate cutting-edge solutions to stay competitive.

These partnerships can potentially enhance service capabilities and facilitate expansion into new markets. Through such developments, these collaborations have a higher potential for ensuring continued growth and relevance in a rapidly changing industry.

Assessing the Growing Collaboration within Ecosystems

The present mobility industry is evolving into a coordinated, ecosystem-based market. It is becoming a place where ventures recently centered around specific regions progressively extend their operations through broader organizations.

These businesses are expanding their services, increasing customer engagement, and discovering new revenue streams using their technology expertise. Let's take a look at DiDi, for instance.

DiDi: The Art of Mobility Integration Mastery

DiDi stands out as a prime example of successful ecosystem integration. DiDi, a ride-sharing service, has expanded to include e-bikes and self-driving taxis, effectively reaching new market segments.

It responded to the increasing need for flexible last-mile transportation solutions by introducing e-bike sharing. Integrating these bikes into its existing app, DiDi facilitates easy transitions between transportation modes. As a result, it accommodates quick, short-distance trips that help alleviate city congestion.

Moreover, DiDi is pioneering the development of autonomous taxis. In turn, signifying its commitment to the next generation of mobility technologies. Thanks to this initiative, the company is now at the forefront of the industry, ready to adapt to shifting consumer preferences and regulatory frameworks. This essential expansion expands DiDi's administration scope and fortifies its situation as a critical member in metropolitan transportation arrangements.

Uber: Growing Past Ridesharing

Beyond traditional ridesharing, Uber has expanded into food delivery with Uber Eats and freight logistics with Uber Freight by utilizing its established platform (we'll delve into this deeper later in the following chapters).

Uber Eats utilizes its vast network of drivers and robust tech infrastructure. That's how Uber has successfully branched out into the competitive food delivery market. The Uber app's familiarity and seamless service delivery optimize user experience, driving growth and diversifying revenue.

Uber Freight, on the other hand, is the product of Uber's adaptation of its on-demand transportation model to the freight industry. It simplifies logistics, connecting truck drivers directly with shipping needs. This service revolutionizes freight by enhancing operational efficiency and offering unprecedented flexibility for shippers and carriers.

The strategic expansions of DiDi and Uber illustrate several critical insights for the mobility industry. The most forward-thinking transportation companies merge various services into a cohesive platform. This strategy not only improves user convenience but also opens up multiple channels for revenue.

Growth and scale are essential for long-term success in the passenger transportation sector. Providers should aim to grow vertically and horizontally, expanding their existing operations while integrating new lines of business. By leveraging technology, they can drive this growth efficiently, enhancing their core services while diversifying their offerings to meet evolving market demands.

Agility and Adaptability in the Passenger Transportation Sector

Throughout the assessment of ongoing developments, agility and flexibility remain the most profitable characteristics and fundamental necessities for achieving enduring success in the highly competitive transportation sector.

The strategies that led providers to their current success will not necessarily take them to the next level. Companies like Blockbuster, Kodak, and Sony Ericsson were once market leaders but failed to recognize how emerging technologies could disrupt their industries. Their rigid structures, resistance to change, and belief that decades of success made them invincible ultimately led to their downfall. This serves as a reminder that adaptability is crucial and that past achievements do not guarantee future success.

The response of TNCs to the COVID-19 pandemic is yet another example that shows the critical significance of adaptability in maintaining operations in the face of unprecedented obstacles. Their businesses quickly implemented new safety measures like mandatory mask policies, in-app health checklists, and enhanced vehicle sanitation procedures.

These measures were necessary for the safety of passengers and drivers and allowed businesses to adapt to changing passenger needs and public health guidelines. For instance, Uber accelerated the expansion of its delivery services in response to the pandemic's decrease in passenger demand. As home delivery became more critical than ever, Uber Eats saw significant growth. This demonstrated its ability to adapt its business model to changing market conditions.

Proactive Regulatory Engagement: Navigating the Evolving Landscape

I also found that exploring the complex administrative climate isn't just about consistency — it's tied with drawing proactively with policymakers to shape the eventual fate of the business.

Organizations like Tesla and TNCs represent how dynamic administrative commitment can be an essential resource for adjusting new regulations and principles in the industry. What's more interesting is that it also highlights the impact on the operational environment. That marks the effects of an innovative development-oriented framework.

Tesla's proactive approach to administrative commitment is apparent in its authority on electric vehicle (EV) well-being and natural principles. Tesla vehicles are known for their high well-being evaluations, accomplished through cutting-edge, dynamic security highlights and hearty vehicle plans.

For instance, Tesla has worked with different administrative bodies to advocate for the impetus for EV purchasers. Take charging discounts and awards, for example, to speed up the shift toward reasonable transportation.

TNCs have also changed metropolitan portability, exploring many administrative difficulties across various urban communities and nations. As part of their proactive regulatory strategies, they work with local governments to develop policies encouraging ride-sharing growth while addressing urban issues like pollution and traffic congestion. They have participated in conversations with city authorities to create assigned rideshare pickup zones in jam-packed metropolitan regions. This would assist with lessening gridlock and further developing security for drivers and travelers.

The lessons learned from pioneers like Tesla and Transportation Network Companies (TNCs) are invaluable for new and emerging entrepreneurs in the passenger transportation sector. Their journey highlights the critical importance of adaptability and flexibility—essential for both startups and established players in the mobility sector. By studying these innovators, aspiring business leaders can better navigate challenges and capitalize on opportunities in this rapidly evolving industry.

Chapter 6
The Big Picture:
Why Macroscopic Trends Are Reshaping Mobility's Future

"Coming together is a beginning; keeping together is progress; working together is success."

-Henry Ford

The evolving urban landscapes in modern cities and emerging economies thrive on a wider mobility concept. It signifies a broader aspect of urban transportation beyond movement from one destination to the next. Mobility in metropolitan areas catalyzes economic, technological, and social advancement, serving as a cohesive bond to environmental sustainability with ongoing developments.

As modernized cities expand and populations increase, technological advancements and economic shifts reshape traditional transportation models. Societal and consumer behaviors in the passenger transportation sector also significantly impact the shifting paradigms of traditional mobility.

The idea of mobility goes beyond practicality, mixing innovation with the promise to redefine urban lifestyles for growing and diversified populations. The previous chapters expanded on introducing autonomous vehicles with electric charging and other sustainability-driven features to integrate with existing transportation networks. They highlighted how these initiatives impacted commute times, inclusivity, and accessibility to bring transformative changes in the mobility landscape.

Understanding the Significance of Mobility

Mobility is pivotal to urban development and societal progress. At its core, it facilitates the movement of people from one place to another, as well as goods, services, and ideas. It underpins the curation and development of an interconnected ecosystem that drives economic productivity. The efficiency of the transportation system in a city directly influences the interconnectivity of businesses, customers, residents, and essential services.

Furthermore, democratizing access to diverse mobility solutions promotes inclusivity to ensure equitable opportunities for all members of society, within and near cities, with a developing mobility landscape. From a macroscopic view, sustainability mobility paves the way for mitigation strategies to reduce environmental impact through cleaner and healthier urban environments while ensuring equitable opportunities.

This chapter explores interconnected ecosystems and how they can improve quality of life, foster sustainable urban development through data-driven strategies, increase equitable opportunities, and innovative designs with real case studies and factual reports.

Economic, Technological, and Societal Shifts Affecting Mobility

In a modern urban landscape, passenger transportation providers witness monumental changes in the mobility industry based on economic dynamics, technological innovations, and societal behavior changes. These factors influence the availability and development of innovative mobility solutions, reshaping how we perceive passenger transportation today.

Technological Innovations

The rapid advancement with an ever-expanding capacity for innovation in the mobility industry was possible through technological interventions. New developments in diverse tech areas have enabled a more accessible, efficient, and secure mobility industry. Numerous technological advancements had a transformative impact on the transportation system.

The rise of autonomous vehicles (AVs) was a significant breakthrough in the automotive and mobility industries. It depicted a more capable technological infrastructure within the evolving economies worldwide, although mostly limited to developing countries. AVs are similar to EVs, which are electric vehicles, but with the inclusion of artificial intelligence-assisted driving technology.

AVs leverage IoT and interconnected sensor technologies to navigate roadways and offer transportation autonomy with increased convenience. Ongoing development in the

AV field promises enhanced safety. With AI-enabled autonomous driving, there is a higher chance of reduced traffic congestion due to streamlined route planning and transportation operations in urban environments.

In Phoenix, Waymo, a leader in AV technology, conducted several trials across the city to demonstrate the advancements in passenger safety and operational efficiency of autonomous vehicles.[21] The city-scale trials and testing raised awareness surrounding the transportation efficiency possible through AVs.

Therefore, the global adoption of AV is expected to increase steadily in the coming years. The projects indicate that AVs will be integrated significantly into urban areas by 2030. According to a report by McKinsey & Company, AVs can reduce traffic accidents by 90%. As a result, it can save billions of dollars spent on healthcare and emergency medical services associated with road accidents while lowering insurance costs.[22]

AI advancement in mobility has picked up pace, playing a pivotal role in optimizing transportation networks and improving user experiences. Leveraging AI-driven algorithms, transportation service providers perform real-time traffic pattern analysis for optimal route planning. With predictive analytics models, the mobility sector benefits

---

[21] https://iieta.org/journals/ijtdi/paper/10.18280/ijtdi.070301
[22] https://www.mckinsey.com/industries/automotive-and-assembly/our-insights/autonomous-drivings-future-convenient-and-connected

from dynamic adjustments to traffic signals based on traffic frequency, vehicle density, and other factors.

In Singapore, cities have conducted widespread implementation of AI-powered traffic management systems. According to a source, it has reduced congestion and smoother traffic values, which experts argue leads to lower stress, commute time, and transportation expenditures for the general population.[23]

The mobility industry continuously makes significant breakthroughs with AI integration and autonomous technologies. It transforms traditional mobility services while challenging existing transportation models that serve passenger transportation needs in urban environments. It also influences public transit vs. private vehicle ownership archetypes across countries.

On the other hand, Mobility-as-a-Service (MaaS) is gaining prominence as it allows commuters to acquire on-demand mobility services, replacing traditional modes of transportation. It also shifts the commuting experiences, introducing new paradigms for revenue generation in the mobility industry as startups offering MaaS platforms emerge frequently.

MaaS is one of the most influential factors behind the popularity of ridesharing platforms, which promotes environmental sustainability as commuters share different

---

[23]https://www.lta.gov.sg/content/dam/ltagov/getting_around/driving_in_sin gapore/intelligent_transport_systems/pdf/smartmobility2030.pdf

modes of transportation through a single digital interface to reduce vehicle emissions and urban congestion.[24]

Economic Implications

Profound changes are unfolding in the economic landscape of mobility. Although many transformations are driven by technological innovations, evolving consumer preferences also play a significant role in the future of urban transportation systems.

Recent economic activity indicates that smart mobility solutions are paramount to the success of urban economics. As more cities expand with growing populations, the investment toward innovative and cutting-edge transportation infrastructures increases exponentially. Cities incorporate substantial economic benefits, such as electric vehicles (EVs) and autonomous technologies, into their urban transportation networks.

A study by the International Transport Forum from 2023 highlights that every \$1 invested toward enhancing public transportation with innovative design principles potentially yielded an average of \$4 in economic returns.[25] The returns were through reduced congestion and increased productivity, the World Economic Forum also confirmed.[26]

---

[24]https://www.c40.org/wp-content/uploads/2022/03/C40-Green-and-Healthy-Streets-Declaration_Public-progress-report_Feb-2022.pdf

[25] https://www.itf-oecd.org/sites/default/files/docs/15cpb_self-drivingcars.pdf

[26]https://www.weforum.org/agenda/2019/07/autonomous-vehicles-driverless-cars-public-transport/

In cities like Amsterdam and Copenhagen, investments toward smart mobility solutions that pioneer bike-sharing programs and electric buses have also significantly increased. These initiatives promote sustainable transportation while stimulating economic growth by reeling in mobility-centered and tech-savvy businesses. Moreover, with the execution of ride-sharing initiatives, the average healthcare costs are decreasing due to reduced air pollution, commute-related stress, and traffic congestion.[27]

The surge in investments within the mobility industry is evidence of the economic impact of innovative transportation solutions. More startups are focusing on autonomous technologies and electric vehicle facilities, including venture capital firms increasing funding for innovative mobility solutions that enhance transportation in urban centers while reducing environmental impact.

A PitchBook report published in 2023 indicated that investments in mobility startups exceeded $50 billion worldwide. It reflects the growing investor confidence and increasing venture capital firms' preference toward the mobility sector's growth potential.[28]

In addition to diversifying investments toward mobility solutions, new initiatives and propositions have surfaced in the sector. The arrival of Mobility-as-a-Service (MaaS)

---

[27]https://www.mos.ed.tum.de/fileadmin/w00ccp/ftm/05-Lehre/05-9-Internationale_Studentenprojekte_globalDrive/euMOVE_2021_Report_fun_siz e_compressed.pdf

[28] https://pitchbook.com/news/reports/q3-2023-mobility-tech-report

platforms is redefining metropolitan transportation economics. A MaaS platform can seamlessly integrate various transportation modes and single, user-friendly digital interfaces for passenger convenience.

According to the Helsinki Regional Transport Authority, Helsinki successfully implemented MaaS and drove cost savings for commuters while reducing the city government's overall traveling expenditures.[29]

The economic impact of innovative mobility solutions is profound. It also affects the labor market, creating new job opportunities and attracting startups and professionals in the software development field.

Furthermore, expanding the renewable energy sector and data analytics fields has significant implications for the job market. Companies increasing their specialization in EV manufacturing, AI-assisted navigation systems, and mobility software platforms are looking for a more diverse workforce with tech-savvy professionals adept at these operations. It contributes to the increasing economic resilience and job growth in urban centers due to sustainable mobility solutions.

The economic implications are vast in the mobility industry. From enhancing productivity to reducing environmental costs and fostering job growth, smart mobility solutions drive sustainable economic development in urban centers. With growing investment in sustainable

---

[29] https://doi.org/10.3390/futuretransp3020029

technologies and interconnected mobility systems, the future of transportation looks promising for global communities.

Societal Changes

Consumer demands and preferences have been instrumental in transforming the mobility industry, especially the metropolitan transportation landscape, which is moving toward sustainable models. From on-demand MaaS solutions to consumers, they showcase changing behaviors toward the mobility industry as a society, reshaping the passenger transportation sector.

Recent studies show a notable shift in consumer preferences for transportation options that inherently feature convenience and sustainability. Generation Z and Millennials predominantly influence the move toward eco-friendly transportation models for long and short-distance travel. It has led to a sharp increase in ride-sharing services and public transit compared to the previous generations.[30]

The reports also indicate a growing preference among the younger generations for ride-sharing platforms, hinting at opportunities to implement sustainable transportation models to reduce the environmental impact of travel operations.

Rapid urbanization is another societal factor influencing the evolving mobility sector's economic and technological

---

[30]https://www.mckinsey.com/industries/automotive-and-assembly/our-insights/europes-gen-z-and-the-future-of-mobility

aspects. With rural areas converting to urban centers and bustling cities, along with scaling migration of people to cities in search of economic opportunities and better quality of life, it is also driving changes in mobility transformation.

More people stepping into cities for sustainable living is influencing the rate of urbanization, which directly influences the scale of transformation in the mobility sector. With the cities becoming denser due to widespread migration, road congestion and air pollution are increasing due to increased demand for private vehicle ownership and everyday transportation facilities. This puts pressure on the traditional transportation networks and underutilized or undeveloped mobility infrastructure.

It is expected that over 60% of the global population will be living in urban areas by 2050. This increases the pressure on urban mobility infrastructure to facilitate the transportation demands of the rising population.[31] A data-driven strategy resulting from this unprecedented pressure has led to the development of micro-mobility solutions.

The societal shift to convenient and affordable mobility solutions has led to the development of innovative transportation models that provide electric scooters and bikes to consumers. It presents flexible and sustainable transportation modes for society, especially in cities with

---

[31]https://www.un.org/development/desa/en/news/population/2018-revision-of-world-urbanization-prospects.html

rapid urbanization challenged by growing transportation infrastructure demands.

In cities worldwide, namely Paris and San Francisco, governments have embraced micro-mobility solutions to curb traffic congestion and reduce carbon emissions by providing commuters with first—and last-mile connectivity.[32] The mobility industry continues to be impacted by the shifts in societal behavior toward transportation services.

With the growing digitalization of resources and access to online platforms with AI-enabled analytics, consumers have comprehensive digital interfaces to plan and optimize routes daily. The availability of TNC'0s platforms is a prime example, as they offer real-time data analytics to commuters so they can plan their journeys more efficiently.

Optimized routes and pre-planned journeys reduce waiting times, which automatically leads to reduced overall travel expenditures and commute satisfaction. With the integration of AI and machine learning capabilities in sustainable transportation management systems, consumers can benefit from better predictive capabilities and operational efficiency in the mobility sector.[33] These facilities are available to commuters through smartphone applications, as seen in the growing ride-sharing service market. Further, data indicates a decline in car ownership

---

[32] https://rosap.ntl.bts.gov/view/dot/63270/dot_63270_DS1.pdf
[33] https://www2.deloitte.com/us/en/blog/business-operations-room-blog/2024/generative-ai-in-transportation-management.html

preferences among the urban populations as consumers increasingly prefer shared mobility services with alternative and, often, sustainable transportation modes. This shift is due to several reasons, including rising living costs and environmental and individual health concerns in urban environments.[34]

The Role of Interconnected Ecosystems in Enhancing Metropolitan Mobility

Interconnected systems operating within the metropolitan mobility landscape fundamentally function on advanced technology such as AI and Machine Learning (ML), cutting-edge IT infrastructure, evolving consumer behaviors, and societal demands. The intertwining of these critical factors significantly impacts the mobility industry, affecting the efficiency and sustainability of inclusive and affordable public transit facilities.

Adaptive and interconnected ecosystems in the mobility industry streamline movement in urban centers and suburbs. The interconnected nature of these systems powered by robust data-driven frameworks enables synergetic collaboration to shape upcoming mobility solutions.

Interconnected ecosystems are integrated passenger transportation networks where the population utilizes different transportation modes that easily connect with and are supported by the cities' and counties' digital

---

[34]https://www.researchgate.net/publication/306187731_The_impact_of_car sharing_on_household_vehicle_ownership

infrastructure and data-sharing platforms. They enhance mobility efficiency by ensuring equitable access to inclusive and sustainable passenger transportation services. These systems are also vital for improving user experience, as is the case of ride-sharing providers.

Dynamic cities worldwide, mostly in developed or developing regions, adopt interconnected mobility ecosystems to address public transit, microtransit challenges, and consumer demand. Challenges like access to affordable and convenient transportation have increased the pressure on authorities to ramp up initiatives that focus on enhancing the efficiency and availability of transportation services to the expanding populations.

A case study by the Lee Kuan Yew School of Public Policy highlighted the significance of Singapore's Smart Nation program, launched by the Singapore Land Transport Authority, to integrate public transit with autonomous vehicles and smart traffic management systems.[35] It led to mobility optimization, ensuring access to convenient and sustainable public transit facilities for the general population.

Experts reviewed Singapore's Smart Nation initiative and reported a noticeable decline in traffic congestion, leading to increased road safety and sustainable transportation operations. The expert review also indicated the utilization of AI-assisted real-time data analytics

---

[35]https://lkyspp.nus.edu.sg/docs/default-source/case-studies/singapores-smart-nation-initiative-final_112018.pdf?sfvrsn=354e720a_2

functionalities to enhance mobility optimization to meet transportation needs while ensuring environmental sustainability with scalability.

The interconnected nature of traffic management data and consumer behavior enables an information-driven mobility transformation to help authorities meet public transportation needs via optimal solutions that increase cost-efficiency and quality of life in urban environments without overburdening limited government resources.

In Barcelona, Spain, the Superblock Project aimed to design city streets to achieve more pedestrian-friendly zones than traditional roads and urban transportation facilities.[36] The increase in pedestrian-friendly zones increased the capacity for walking and cycling among urban populations, thereby reducing the environmental impact and shifting the paradigm from private vehicle ownership to sustainable mobility solutions.[37]

The Superblock Project, launched in 2017 despite attempts as early as 1993, was first initiated in the Poble Nou district.[38] Reports indicate that the project was met with resistance from businesses and motorists. Similarly, the report also confirms that during the initial phases, the general population in the district showed reluctance to adopt the idea. Therefore, the authorities in Barcelona, Spain,

---

[36] https://www.sciencedirect.com/science/article/pii/S0160412019315223

[37] https://www.c40.org/case-studies/barcelona-superblocks/

[38] https://www.iaa-mobility.com/en/newsroom/news/urban-mobility/superblocks-for-everyone#:~:text=After%20initial%20attempts,for%20sustainable%20mobility.

optimized the project guidelines for effective strategy implementation to encourage adoption among district residents.[39]

Within a few years, the initial superblock was successful, leading to more superblocks around the bustling city. Currently, there are nearly 509 superblocks under planning to meet the sustainable mobility goals of the town.[40] Superblocks are expected to increase the population's environmental, health, and economic benefits. As it will lead to limited vehicular access to promote active mobility, it can encourage healthier urban lifestyles and improved air quality due to reduced carbon emissions.

The interconnectivity of transportation modes with data-driven IT infrastructures for efficient mobility service management in dynamic cities enhances efficiency. It leads to seamless integration of transportation modes with commuter-first digital interfaces or smartphone applications to reduce travel times. Commuters benefit from data-powered algorithms to benefit from optimize route planning, which leads to reduced congestion while also decreasing the probability and frequency of rush hours.

Furthermore, the interconnectedness of urban mobility models paves the way for proactive safety measures. For instance, optimized traffic management with data analytics

---

[39]https://diposit.ub.edu/dspace/bitstream/2445/131499/1/Nota%20Lluis%20Torrens_2Eng.pdf

[40]https://www.who.int/news-room/feature-stories/detail/barcelona-using-urban-design-to-improve-urban-health

powers real-time collision avoidance systems. Additionally, fast-traffic data processing systems increase emergency response coordination during collision detection and incident reporting.

According to the European Commission, city smart traffic management systems reported a noticeable decline in traffic accidents, especially traffic-associated fatalities and life-altering injuries.[41] Simultaneously, the decreasing reliance on single-occupancy vehicles and private car ownership with the rapid increase in shared transportation services has been credited to the developing interconnected mobility ecosystems.

Ride-sharing facilities and convenient route planning with on-demand transportation services enable urban populations to reduce dependence on private vehicle traveling. As a result, it can lead to reduced carbon emissions with fewer single-occupancy vehicles like cars on the roads, further mitigating the greenhouse gas effects in urban areas for healthier living environments and improved air quality. Several studies have confirmed a direct correlation between increased public transit usage and reduced greenhouse gas emissions.[42] [43]

---

[41] https://www.eca.europa.eu/ECAPublications/SR-2024-04/SR-2024-04_EN.pdf

[42] https://www.apta.com/wpcontent/uploads/Resources/resources/reportsand publications/Documents/greenhouse_brochure.pdf

[43] https://www.wri.org/insights/current-state-of-public-transport-climate-goals

Integrated Transportation Networks in Metropolitan Mobility Landscape

In addition to the ongoing developments aimed at promoting ride-sharing convenience in urban centers, there is growing emphasis on the efficiency gains derived from such services. Inclusive ride-sharing models improved interconnected mobility within urban centers and suburbs to reduce commute time significantly. Since passengers will be more likely to increase their reliance on hailed-mobility trips around cities, it reduces the potential traffic congestion.

A study confirms that this interconnectedness through smart mobility solutions can support cost savings for commuters while increasing their productivity. However, advancing the interconnected ecosystem of public transit in metropolitan environments translates to higher economic benefits and the potential to boost private sector activity.

According to a Science Direct Study, smart mobility solutions in cities can lead to lower per-km energy consumption, enhancing sustainability-driven transportation initiatives' effectiveness.[44] Furthermore, the research also confirms that energy savings are achieved by users' increasing reliance on smart mobility solutions as they travel less. When they do, they opt for convenient and environmentally friendly transit facilities.

Based on the European Court of Auditors study from April 2019, a 10% reduction in commute time can lead to a

---

[44]https://www.sciencedirect.com/science/article/pii/S1361920916306228?via%3Dihub

productivity boost of around 2.9%.[45] The study reveals those statistics for highly congested regions, assuming that free-flowing traffic could lead to a productivity increase of up to 30%. It highlights inefficient mobility solutions, costing the EU member states around €110 billion annually, equivalent to 1% of the EU's GDP.

Environmental sustainability becomes a by-product when integrated transportation networks are implemented widely across urban centers. With the suggested reduction in traffic congestion incidents and enhanced road safety with reduced commute time, leading to cost and energy savings on a macro level, interconnectedness promotes eco-friendly traveling. It leads to fewer unnecessary miles traveled as a result.

To fully utilize the interlinked data and technology infrastructure to enhance urban mobility, integrated planning, and innovation-driven solutions play a vital role. Through collaboration between the public and private sectors to incentivize sustainable mobility solutions, governments can pave the way for resilient metropolitan structures built on smart transportation management and service delivery frameworks.

The Democratization of Access to Mobility Solutions

One of the growing concerns in pursuing sustainable mobility solutions is ensuring equitable access to eco-friendly transportation services. It is the cornerstone of

---

[45]https://www.eca.europa.eu/lists/ecadocuments/ap19_07/ap_urban_mobilit y_en.pdf

societal progress, especially in urban development for energy-efficient mobility services. This section will explore the democratization of access to advanced mobility solutions to enhance convenience, social inclusion, and sustainability development for commuters.

We will examine how several initiatives aim to bridge the widening gap between underserved population segments in metropolitan and rural areas, and the ongoing mobility service development by addressing the underlying socio-economic factors. By doing so, cities worldwide strive to turn eco-friendly transportation from a privilege to a fundamental economic and societal development right. This section will explore the benefits of ride-sharing platforms and how they reach underserved communities to promote eco-friendly transportation options among various population segments. The power of inclusive mobility strategies reveals underlying potential for more resilient and interconnected environments.

Democratization primarily involves ensuring access to mobility solutions, including transportation services as affordable and accessible basic rights for all socio-economic groups. With equitable access granted across various income groups differentiated through socioeconomic factors, cities plan to overcome mobility barriers, which can also create the capacity for testing and deploying more efficient transportation solutions to meet growing sustainability demands.

Public-Private Sector Collaboration to Increase Access to Cost-Effective Mobility Solutions

Consumer partners like TNCs have already ventured into the niche segment where consumers with disabilities are catered to for their transportation needs. TNCs Access have been providing wheel-chair-accessible vehicles (WAVs), transforming the ride-sharing mobility service landscape. With specialized transportation facilities available to people with disabilities, the mobility ecosystem moves toward greater resilience and all-inclusivity.

Transportation initiatives targeting accessibility enhancement in cities aren't limited to private ride-sharing providers. The recent developments have ushered the public-private sector into a new era of collaboration where city governments team up with ride-sharing providers to subsidize transportation costs for low-income residents. This monumental initiative marked a significant move toward incorporating the transportation needs of low-income groups, primarily in the lower socioeconomic bracket.

Los Angeles Metro partnered with TNCs to subsidize rides for its residents to transit hubs and essential services around the underserved neighborhoods.[46] With cost-effective transportation options through widely accessible ride-sharing platforms, commuters can save time and money, leading to more conscious spending. While there is little evidence to support that, there is a higher potential for

---

[46]https://www.apta.com/research-technical-resources/mobility-innovation-hub/transit-and-tnc-partnerships/

enhanced urban mobility with widespread adoption of subsidized transportation models with public-private sector collaboration.

Emergence of Micro-Mobility Solutions for Urban Development

Micro-mobility solutions emerged as a multi-faceted tool for urban development. While ensuring cost-effective transit across city centers, micro-mobility transportation options also ensure sustainable urban movement. Several government initiatives in smart cities worldwide promote and encourage bike-sharing platforms and electric scooters.

The authorities plan to advertise these transportation options as affordable and flexible mobility choices for a more resilient and adaptive population.

In France, Paris' Vélib' Métropole is one of the first initiatives to launch low-cost bike rentals and integrate them with public transit networks to democratize access to affordable and convenient transportation facilities. [47] The smart city, Paris, is already among the leading urban centers in the world that actively develop, implement and advocate intelligent traffic management and innovative sustainability-driven mobility solutions. The initiative aims to improve first and last-mile connectivity for greener transportation operations across the city.

---

[47] https://www.velib-metropole.fr/en/service

With the onset of micro-mobility solutions, initiatives like Paris' Vélib' Métropole also incorporated sustainability-centered frameworks for delivering transportation services to the public. The electricity-powered vehicles, EVs, are steadily transforming the public transit infrastructure in modern cities. Subsidies facilitated the adoption of electric cars and have been instrumental in advancing zero-emission zones across smart cities.

One example is the City of Oslo, where EV owners and ride-sharing services are offered free parking and toll exemptions to encourage greener transportation activities.[48] This not only incentivizes the move from private vehicle ownership and increased greenhouse emissions but presents them as affordable and convenient alternatives to traditional transportation options.

On the other hand, the City of Portland adopted initiatives like "SmartTrips," where the government encourages commuters to walk, cycle, and carpool to reduce dependency on single-occupancy vehicles. The city government developed test projects to improve pedestrian infrastructure and allocate bike lanes on the busiest roads. The initiatives aimed to enhance safety and encourage activity mobility choices focused on improving the population's overall health and fitness levels.

While ongoing studies remain inconclusive in confirming the effects of micro- and active-mobility transportation

---

[48] https://www.ncbi.nlm.nih.gov/pmc/articles/PMC10935741/

options, it is ascertained that such initiatives remain effective strategies in addressing the rising demands for eco-friendly and cost-effective transit facilities.[49]

Further studies highlight the environmental benefits of adopting sustainable mobility practices, such as transitioning from traditional transportation models to electronic vehicles. While this also necessitates setting up strategic EV charging ports and centers across smart cities, it creates a demand-driven groundwork for a sustainable urban transportation infrastructure.

The transition to EV vehicles and increasing public transit usage significantly impact greenhouse gas emissions, leading to noticeable reductions in air pollution and improved air quality. The effects are more prominent in urban areas as cities continue to implement comprehensive mobility strategies with measurable indicators that highlight the reduction in the carbon footprint of transportation activity.[50]

A major example is London's Ultra Low Emission Zone (ULEZ), which has contributed to a significant reduction of nearly 20% in nitrogen oxide emissions inside the city center.[51] Sustainable transportation solutions can potentially

---

[49]https://www.portland.gov/sites/default/files/2021/2030-bicycle-plan-progress-report_final_1.pdf

[50]https://theicct.org/wp-content/uploads/2023/11/ID-22-%E2%80%93-1.5-C-strategies-report-A4-65005-v8.pdf

[51] https://www.gov.uk/government/statistics/transport-and-environment-statistics-2023/transport-and-environment-statistics-2023

help substantially reduce carbon emissions across other regions.[52]

The Impact on Quality of Life with Human-Centric Mobility Solution Designs

The focus on human-centric design has increased exponentially in recent years as the underserved and underprivileged population segments become part of the broad transportation service coverage. The availability of ride-sharing and other sustainable mobility alternatives primarily erupts from human-centric designs. The main goal of a human-centric approach in designing and delivering eco-friendly transportation services to the general public is to enhance safety, accessibility, and user experience with increased comfort.

In Denmark's capital, Copenhagen, the government adopted a forward-thinking approach to integrate the existing urban infrastructure with pedestrian-friendly planning to ensure pedestrian and cyclist safety. The city went through extensive research and comprehensive planning to set test projects in motion with investments in additional sidewalks, dedicated bike lanes, and pedestrian-only zones that restrict the movement of vehicles to improve air quality and traffic's free flow.

As a result, this human-centric urban design has reduced traffic congestion and drastically improved the overall

---

[52] https://tfl.gov.uk/corporate/about-tfl/air-quality

atmosphere in the pedestrian-only zones, with better air quality and measurable reductions in carbon emissions.

Commuter-Specific Safety Standards and Improved Convenience

In Singapore, the Mass Rapid Transit (MRT) adopted a range of design features to enhance the accessibility of public transit to the population. Including step-free access and tactile flooring was a milestone achievement to ensure access to wheelchair-enabled and special needs commuters. On the other hand, audio-visual announcements played a pivotal role in addressing the diverse needs of commuters, especially those with hearing or visual impairment.

The elderly population also benefitted significantly from the universal design features to enhance mobility in urban planning.[53] Similarly, the previously mentioned Superblock initiative in Barcelona, Spain, promotes car-free zones. It offers multi-faceted benefits for the urban mobility ecosystem, reducing car accident incidences and enhancing commuter safety. Furthermore, reduced dependency on single-occupancy vehicles in these dedicated areas also improves air quality as there are significant reductions in carbon emissions.

The reports also indicate that reduced private car ownership might potentially impact the dependence on fossil

---

[53]https://www.lta.gov.sg/content/ltagov/en/getting_around/public_transport/a_better_public_transport_experience/an_inclusive_public_transport_system.html

fuels. The presence of dedicated pedestrian-only and car-free zones is a factor that contributes directly to social inclusivity as the population is encouraged to take up walkability as a core part of their daily routine. With long-term physical health implications and social interactions, the overall atmosphere could serve as a coherent force behind driving sustainable transportation alternatives.

The European Environment Agency indicates that increased pedestrian movement through walking, cycling, and electric vehicle transit contributes to reduced particulate matter and nitrogen dioxide emissions in the environment.[54] As a result, this enhances air quality, positively impacting the population's overall health.

Since it is proved through scientific research and extensive studies that improved air quality plays a critical role in impacting the prevalence of respiratory health conditions and associated risks,[55] Modern sustainability alternatives receive increasing support from advocacy groups and government authorities alike.[56]

Human-centric mobility solutions have also shown observable improvements in quality-of-life indicators. For instance, several European cities reported significant improvements in the happiness index and community

---

[54] https://www.eea.europa.eu/publications/europes-air-quality-status-2023
[55] https://www.who.int/news-room/fact-sheets/detail/ambient-(outdoor)-air-quality-and-health
[56] https://www.sciencedirect.com/science/article/pii/S0048969723049653

engagement rates due to sustainable transportation alternatives.[57]

Currently, the landscape of the mobility industry is undergoing major transformations aimed at improving sustainability-driven public transportation infrastructure in smart cities with plans to initiate similar projects in developing regions. The future of mobility promises continued innovation and adaptive frameworks for implementing eco-friendly transportation modes for the general public.

However, the imperative for strategic planning and incentivizing cutting-edge mobility innovations remains a cornerstone for realizing effective change in the urban mobility landscape. With real-world social, economic, and technological implications, the urban mobility infrastructure tilts in both directions. By overcoming challenges and addressing the growing need for robust infrastructures through strategic investments, equitable access to environmentally friendly mobility solutions can be guaranteed across developed city centers worldwide.

We have explored numerous examples illustrating how the mobility industry influences our day-to-day experiences—some with immediate effects and others that unfold over time. These observations make one thing clear: the passenger transportation sector is at a pivotal juncture, requiring a redefinition that keeps pace with these

---

[57]https://ec.europa.eu/regional_policy/sources/reports/qol2023/2023_qualit y_life_european_cities_en.pdf

transformative shifts. In the next chapter, we'll look at how transportation is evolving, reshaping itself to meet the demands of a rapidly changing world. Prepare to uncover the forces driving this revolution and what they mean for the future of mobility as we know it.

Chapter 7
Redefining Passenger Transportation: Why the Future Demands a Bold New Approach

"The only way to discover the limits of the possible is to go beyond them into the impossible."

-Arthur C. Clarke

Passenger Transportation was once a means of getting from one point to the next. Today, it catalyzes metropolitan development and economic growth. It is the means to connect not just two places or provide a way for people to travel but also bridge ideas and gaps between nations worldwide.

Through metropolitan development, and modern transportation systems, mobility solutions have evolved beyond the traditional definitions. As societies embrace new technologies, transportation is becoming more valued for its functional role and its implications on other economic, technological, and societal factors. It is changing lifestyles and aligning with the evolving environmental priorities across the public and private sectors.

In the past, it was focused on the efficient movement of people. The primary goal was to move reliably and quickly. However, that has changed significantly as the goals have expanded to include safety, cost-efficiency, and adaptability as core components of efficient travel. Modern-day transportation is a crucial factor in addressing urban dynamics and the personal mobility preferences of consumers, all while complying with sustainability efforts.

The new demands and technological advances have led to cutting-edge transportation infrastructure that has redefined the mobility industry. These modern advancements have been pivotal in shaping the future of passenger transportation as we perceive it today, making it increasingly more sophisticated and adaptive to meet changing consumer needs.

Here, we will explore how passenger transportation evolved over the decades. Most importantly, we will examine the main factors redefining the transportation sector and introducing new transit facilities that defy historical definitions. We will also discuss the importance and integrational value of advanced mobility design principles that have helped governments and the private sector develop cutting-edge technologies.

Today's transportation is different from what the previous generations perceived. Going back a few decades gives a different outlook on transit facilities. However, we have embraced innovation and groundbreaking technologies to bolster the connectivity models in urban models. Modern transportation is now a facilitator of movement and a catalyst for economic growth. It also impacts the quality of life and significantly enhances people's lifestyles.

We will also overview research and case studies that prove the evolving mobility landscape in the context of metropolitan planning and shifting consumer preferences. It will provide valuable insights regarding the dynamic changes in the passenger transportation sector.

Examining the Traditional Perspective and Purpose of Modern Transportation

Transportation has undergone tremendous changes over the years. From moving people to catalyzing metropolitan development, it has also introduced remarkable opportunities and challenges within the sector. However, the modern purpose of transportation defies the traditional perspectives that confined the function and facilities of the mobility industry.

While collective travel had always been necessary, modern transportation defied historical definitions by influencing global economics. Throughout history, transportation was a means to travel – and that was it. The Industrial Revolution was a watershed moment that sparked innovation in transportation, leading to faster and more efficient technologies that we witness today.

The development of expansive canal networks and steam-powered trains underpinned the contemporary innovation in mobility. The revolution impacted global connectivity and led to unexpected economic growth, further boosting the groundwork for modern transportation infrastructure.

As a result, the traditional needs of moving people across greater distances quickly and more efficiently were met with unprecedented changes. The early 20th century witnessed the large-scale development and manufacturing of automobiles, further cementing the newly streamlined mobility industry's progress with widespread adoption. The availability of automobiles as personal mobility systems became a symbol of freedom, aligning with the liberty values of developing nations.

They were also indicators of an affluent population segment or individual. As the utilization of mobility systems like personal automobiles increased, it led to suburban area developments and boosted urban planning strategies worldwide. As a result, we witnessed growing urbanization to meet the evolving needs for a better quality of life augmented with the availability of efficient and personal-use transportation systems.

Historical developments have influenced societies and economic growth factors for decades. Meanwhile, public transportation was further boosted by the advancements in air travel. It increased global interconnectedness, and as industry leaders pioneered international commerce solutions and tourism facilities, air travel became even more lucrative.

Similarly, sea travel evolved in response to technological innovations and societal needs, from rowing boats to steamers and gigantic cruise ships that were big enough to house a significant portion of a small city's population. The main factors behind the redefining evolution of the mobility industry were societal needs and tech innovations, leading us into the present era of mobility solutions.

An Overview of Modern-Day Transportation and Challenges

In this century, transportation has come across epoch-defining innovations and pioneering changes that make movement efficient and environmentally friendly. However, it has also introduced many challenges due to rapid urbanization and environmental sustainability initiatives. The society expects the public and private sector leaders to embrace new mobility solutions that solve issues like escalating traffic congestion and deteriorating air quality.

Meanwhile, the already strained transportation infrastructure presents severe obstacles to overcoming these challenges and meeting the rapidly expanding population's mobility needs. Regardless, the challenges necessitate and catalyze innovation, improving overall efficiency, sustainability, and accessibility of metropolitan and rural mobility solutions.

Today's commuters demand seamless transit facilities, which are possible through an integrated transportation system supervised by adaptive performance monitoring and evaluation models. Societal expectations have shifted from the mere availability of common transportation modes to environmental responsibility and affordability. The growing emphasis on reducing the carbon footprint of transportation activities is raising the bar for modern mobility service providers to address global climate goals.

It also increases the pressure on equitable access to transportation services, which remains a critical issue with rising disparities due to economic and societal factors in underdeveloped or developing regions. Consumers plan to receive convenient and affordable mobility services that promote sustainable travel options. In hindsight, it also meets the growing demand for improved air quality in urban centers, primarily characterized by frequent traffic congestion and greenhouse gas emissions due to single-occupancy vehicle activity.

On the other hand, the public and private sectors are increasing collaboration to address the disproportional mobility options facing marginalized communities. Equal transportation options are vital to ensure economic opportunities and social inclusion for various population segments. However, this requires a systematic approach to addressing these inequalities, starting with poor public mobility services and fewer transportation options in the most affected areas.

All these challenges are currently driving the modern mobility industry. It has encouraged urban planners and governments, including transportation experts, to embrace innovative approaches to resolve mobility inequalities facing the growing global population. Smart technologies, integrated public transit networks, micro-mobility solutions, and intelligent traffic management systems are being designed and improved to meet evolving needs worldwide.

Recent Case Studies Highlighting Transformative Shifts in Transportation

Real-world examples have always helped inform and illustrate the transformative impact of innovative solutions in an industry. The mobility industry is no exception, as countless technology-based innovations have boosted public transit facilities globally. However, the primary beneficiaries were populations residing in leading nations regarding technology infrastructure and economic capacity.

The Integrated Public Transport System (SITP) in Bogota, Colombia, pioneered comprehensive initiatives prioritizing public transit over private vehicles, mainly single-occupancy vehicles, which are the major contributors to greenhouse gas emissions and deteriorating air quality in urban centers.[58] It was responsible for launching the TransMilenio Bus Rapid Transit (BRT) system in 2000, which transformed metropolitan mobility.

It effectively reduced commuter travel times and the dependency on single-occupancy vehicles for inter-city travel, which experts argued improved air quality. Moreover, the TransMilenio BRT system was accessible to millions of residents in Bogota, Colombia, demonstrating the impact of sustainable mass transit solutions in a densely populated urban center.[59]

---

[58] https://www.mdpi.com/2071-1050/10/11/3958

[59] https://www.researchgate.net/publication/271915173_The_promise_and_challenges_of_integrating_public_transportation_in_Bogota_Colombia

We have already discussed the micro-mobility solutions in Paris, France, to enhance the sustainability factors of public transportation activities. Options such as electric scooters and bike-sharing programs were designed and made available to the general public to improve air quality. They also reduced traffic congestion and were seen as an increasingly popular sustainability solution to the ongoing urban mobility challenges. Vélib' Métropole, a bike-sharing and rental company in Paris, currently oversees the availability of more than 18,000 vehicles for eco-friendly travel across the city.[60] It also highlighted the significant impact of interconnected user applications and integration transportation management systems by allowing commuters to book or activate electric scooters through a mobile app.

Such initiatives make a valuable and impactful contribution to the private transportation infrastructure and local communities. They also increased awareness about sustainable transportation practices that align with the business's environmental goals.

Furthermore, the shared autonomous shuttle services in Gothenburg, Sweden, helped improve the public transportation network. Residents and visitors to the city had access to innovative and sustainable mobility solutions, and driverless shuttles operated on designated routes. It was a first and last-mile connectivity solution that significantly reduced the traffic situation in the smart city. Moreover, it promoted safety and bolstered Sweden's commitment to

---

[60] https://data.europa.eu/en/publications/use-cases/velib-metropole

embracing cutting-edge public mobility solutions for better and more efficient urban mobility.

The real-world examples demonstrate that the public and private sectors across different nations are collaborating to pioneer solutions in response to modern transportation challenges. The primary influencers behind these innovations are sustainability goals, which have evolved over the past decade, and the increasing consumer demand for convenient, affordable, and inclusive passenger transportation services.

The Integration of Design and Technology for Dynamic Mobility Solutions

Integrating cutting-edge technology to design seamless and dynamic mobility solutions has been increasingly important. Transportation sector leaders have delivered efficient and user-centric mobility solutions by integrating design technology and sustainability frameworks.

The design thinking principles require innovators to pursue human-centric strategies that resolve mobility challenges while meeting commuters' convenience, affordability, and safety expectations. The modern mobility industry has benefitted significantly and continues developing due to sophisticated design-production frameworks that empathize with user needs to create efficient solutions.

Moreover, the importance of design technology is highlighted in prototyping innovations to iterate valuable feedback, which aims to improve and address inconsistencies in passenger transportation solutions. Design thinking has been influential in addressing the accessibility and inclusivity demands of commuters worldwide. This is especially true for transportation options facilitating disabled or underprivileged population segments in smart and developing cities.

Human-centric designs like low-floor buses and trains, reserved spaces with clear signage and priority seating, and tactile indicators have improved mobility services for the disabled population segments.

More importantly, the technology that has enabled these innovative solutions to address various disparities in the transportation sector has evolved remarkably over the years. For now, Artificial Intelligence, augmented by Machine Learning (ML) capabilities, and the Internet of Things (IoT) are two of the most sophisticated technologies responsible for driving innovation in the mobility industry.

Significance of AI and IoT Technologies in Urban Mobility Landscape

AI has revolutionized transportation by redefining it through its ability to process vast amounts of data. It facilitates decision-making by revealing actionable insights and valuable data that promote operational intelligence across industries. In passenger transportation, AI has had several instances where it enabled seamless transportation management and contributed significantly to the overall sustainability efforts of mobility services.

In Singapore and London, as discussed in the previous chapter, AI-powered traffic management systems have reduced traffic congestion and arguably improved the quality of life through reduced greenhouse gas emissions, translating into an improved air quality index for the cities. It was also instrumental in the automobile industry, where autonomous vehicles (AVs) received increasing preference for their environmentally friendly benefits compared to traditional, high-GHG single-occupancy vehicles.

AI has been pivotal in improving automated traffic management operations in smart cities. For example, the Olympic Autonomous Shuttle Service in Tokyo made it possible to increase the utilization of electric shuttles with AI navigation systems through improved sensor and navigation capabilities.[61]

The autonomous shuttles provided efficient transportation for athletes, spectators, and officials. They navigated designated areas as safe and reliable mobility solutions.[62] Although in their initial stages, the cutting-edge features set the foundation for better and more capable autonomous vehicle systems to facilitate major sporting events in urban centers.

The Internet of Things (IoT) technology, which ensures connectivity between physical devices and systems, enabled

---

[61]https://olympics.com/ioc/news/toyota-s-innovative-mobility-solutions-taking-olympic-transport-to-new-heights-in-tokyo

[62]https://www.bloomberg.com/news/newsletters/2021-08-02/toyota-seizes-olympic-glory-by-shuttling-athletes-autonomously

a seamless integration of interconnected transportation networks with real-time data infrastructures. Through integration with data exchange across multiple transportation networks within an urban center, IoT enables more efficient and environmentally friendly urban mobility planning.[63]

The smart sensors from the IoT ecosystem integrate seamlessly with the vast public mobility infrastructure to collect real-time data about air quality, infrastructure conditions, vehicle capacity, and traffic flow. It is part of a comprehensive data-driven approach to urban mobility planning and solutions delivery.

IoT systems have enabled more seamless parking across significant cities with real-time information on which parking spaces are available or ready for use to reduce traffic congestion and improve fuel efficiency.[64] In Paris, the private sector launched Autolib,' an electric car-sharing service, as a collaboration between Velib,' the city's bike-sharing system, and Bolloré, a French conglomerate.[65] According to Wikipedia, Autolib' was a *"fleet of all-electric Bolloré Bluecars for public use on a paid subscription basis."*[66]

Although the program was terminated due to financial constraints, it laid the groundwork for efficient car parking,

---

[63]https://www.researchgate.net/publication/360938699_Improvement_of_u rban_mobility_supported_with_IoT_technologies
[64]https://www.sciencedirect.com/science/article/pii/S2667345223000494
[65]https://www.c40.org/case-studies/c40-good-practice-guides-paris-autolib/
[66]https://en.wikipedia.org/wiki/Autolib%27

charging stations, and vehicle management systems for smart mobility solutions in urban centers.[67]

The Continuous Shift to Individual Mobility Preferences

Urban mobility evolved further and redefined passenger transportation with the launch of ride-sharing, micro-mobility, and on-demand transit facilities. TNCs have been major players in the on-demand commute market, offering urban transportation options with convenience and accessibility.

As discussed in the previous chapters, the evolution of urban mobility due to ride-sharing platforms was further bolstered by government subsidies and initiatives, making transportation affordable for designated areas or residents living in specific locations across a city. Reducing transportation fares due to private-public sector collaboration addressed the socio-economic factors limiting economic growth and individual development.

Moreover, technological advancements allowed commuters to switch from collective mobility options to individual mobility solutions using their smartphone application. These apps promoted the availability of on-demand transportation services. With the integration of AVs in the ride-sharing sector, sustainability efforts have reached increased awareness in multiple cities.

---

[67]https://www.reuters.com/article/technology/paris-ends-autolib-electric-car-sharing-contract-with-bollore-idUSKBN1JH2CM/

In addition to adopting AVs for efficient and environmentally friendly travel, individual mobility preferences significantly impacted the availability of affordable services. This led to the development of subscription-based mobility services such as car-sharing, carpooling, and other vehicle subscription platforms.

According to a McKinsey & Company report, the shared mobility industry could generate up to $1 Trillion in consumer spending by 2030.[68] The report further confirms that this increases consumer demand for convenient, affordable transportation solutions.

This further emphasizes the shift from collective to individual mobility preferences, hinting toward the increased likelihood of commuters paying for sustainable on-demand transit facilities. On the other hand, consumers also embrace innovative and purposeful mobility solutions like adopting electric vehicles for reduced carbon footprint through eco-friendly traveling.

The International Energy Agency confirmed that by the end of 2020, the number of active electric vehicles serving as sustainable mobility solutions on the roads in smart cities was estimated to be 10 million.[69] The report also confirmed that electric car sales increased by 140% during the first quarter of 2021 compared to the same period in 2020.

---

[68]https://www.mckinsey.com/industries/automotive-and-assembly/our-insights/shared-mobility-sustainable-cities-shared-destinies
[69]https://www.iea.org/reports/global-ev-outlook-2021

These real-world case studies and insightful statistics reveal that the evolution of transportation is crucial for building inclusive, equitable and sustainable cities. It is vital to meet the evolving consumer demands in the 21st century while meeting global sustainability initiatives.

As we close this chapter, we see that passenger transportation has evolved from simply being a means of transit to becoming a cornerstone of urban development, economic growth, and societal connectivity. The dynamic shifts driven by technology, sustainability goals, and changing consumer preferences have redefined how we view mobility in today's world.

Yet, the transformation does not stop here. The journey continues as we look toward shaping the future of transportation. The next chapter will guide us through the innovations and visions poised to redefine how we move, plan, and interact with the world around us. We will explore groundbreaking technologies, policy shifts, and the role of forward-thinking leaders in paving the way for a new era in mobility. Prepare to envision a future where transportation isn't just efficient and inclusive but becomes a driving force for a more connected, equitable, and sustainable world.

Chapter 8
Shaping the Future:
Why Our Actions Today Will
Define Tomorrow's Mobility

"The best way to predict the future is to create it."

-Peter Drucker

The landscape of mobility is undergoing a profound transformation. It is constantly driven by rapid technological advancements and evolving societal preferences. What was once a straightforward means of getting from point A to B has now evolved into a dynamic ecosystem that seamlessly integrates diverse mobility solutions.

We will explore the pivotal role of cultural shifts and technological innovations in reshaping the current mobility landscape and its future. During the last few years, people have started perceiving and using transportation differently than public transit operations in the previous century or even 10 or 15 years ago.

Traditional transit modes are being complemented and, in some cases, supplanted by personalized mobility services that offer convenience and flexibility tailored to individual needs. Moreover, integrating advanced technologies is revolutionizing mobility, making transportation systems smarter, more efficient, and environmentally sustainable.

The cultural shift based on changing consumer preferences in mobility has significantly impacted the evolution of traditional transportation models. It was influential in aiding the transition to more personalized services due to changing consumer behaviors and lifestyle growth trends.

On the other hand, integrating mobility models highlighted the importance of having a robust, streamlined, and interconnected mobility ecosystem. Integrating such models, from ride-sharing to public transit, in metropolitan planning was a critical driver behind developing seamless transportation ecosystems that continue to influence the day-to-day transportation activities of consumers.

The ongoing emphasis on inclusivity, equitability, sustainability, and innovation has been a guiding principle for transportation development. These interconnected themes are reshaping the transportation landscape and paving the way for a more integrated, efficient, and sustainability-driven future in metropolitan mobility planning and execution.

Cultural Shifts in Transportation

To understand the future of transportation, it is essential to examine how various cultural shifts are reshaping mobility preferences and services. Today, we realize that the evolution from traditional transportation modes to personalized services was a significant development that had implications for our preexisting metropolitan mobility planning processes.

However, the evolution of mobility preferences reflects broader societal changes and technological advancements. Historically, transportation primarily served to efficiently move people from one point to another. With the advent of new technologies and changing lifestyles, the role of transportation expanded beyond mere functionality to encompass convenience, flexibility, and sustainability.

Consumer behavior studies indicate there is a notable shift toward personalized mobility solutions.[70] Today's metropolitan dwellers increasingly prioritize convenience and flexibility in their transportation choices. This shift is evident in the growing adoption of ride-sharing services, which offer on-demand or by reservation access to transportation without the ownership responsibilities associated with traditional modes like private cars.

Moreover, studies show that younger demographics, particularly, are driving the adoption of new mobility solutions.[71] They are more inclined to use ride-sharing and other shared mobility options than owning a vehicle outright. This trend is not only influenced by economic considerations but also by a preference for experiences over ownership.

For instance, a scientific study states that millennials and Generation Z are more likely to use ride-sharing and micro-mobility services than previous generations.[72] This demographic shift underscores a broader cultural change

---

[70]https://www.sciencedirect.com/science/article/pii/S2214629622001001
[71]https://research.tue.nl/files/150350842/TRA2020_VCaiati.pdf
[72]https://www.sciencedirect.com/topics/social-sciences/millennials

where access to mobility is valued over ownership, aligning with sustainable urban development goals.

As cities grow denser and traffic congestion worsens, the appeal of shared mobility solutions continues to rise. These services offer cost-effective alternatives to private car ownership. In addition, they contribute to reducing urban traffic congestion and lowering overall carbon emissions. As a result, urban planners are increasingly integrating these insights into transportation policies to promote sustainable and efficient mobility solutions for their residents.[73]

The Rise of Personalized Mobility Services

The rise of personalized mobility services marked a significant departure from traditional transportation models. Ride-sharing platforms pioneered the concept of on-demand or by-reservation mobility. As a result, it revolutionized how people moved within cities.[74]

Uber, founded in 2009, quickly disrupted the transportation sector by offering a convenient alternative to taxis through its mobile app.[75] Lyft, launched shortly after in 2012, introduced a similar model focusing on community and shared rides. These platforms allow users to request rides at the touch of a button. They provide real-time access to

---

[73]https://www.weforum.org/agenda/2024/05/is-public-mobility-the-next-public-transport-revolution/

[74]https://www.researchgate.net/publication/347629119_A_new_ridesharing _model_incorporating_the_passengers'_efforts

[75] https://www.cascade.app/studies/uber-strategy-study

transportation services tailored to their immediate needs where traditional public transit facilities might often fail.

The growth of on-demand transportation services has been staggering. Statistics reveal that globally, the ride-sharing market is projected to reach billions in revenue by the decade's end, reflecting its rapid expansion and widespread adoption.[76] These services appeal not only to urban commuters but also to travelers and residents in suburban areas seeking flexible transportation options.

For example, Uber's expansion into UberEats illustrates the versatility of these platforms beyond passenger transportation. By leveraging its existing infrastructure and network of drivers, UberEats delivers food directly to customers' doorsteps. This is an advanced integration of mobility models into urban lifestyles.[77]

Furthermore, the adoption rates of ride-sharing services continue to climb. It is driven by convenience, affordability, and environmental considerations. Studies indicate that cities with well-established ride-sharing networks experience reduced congestion and improved air quality. [78] This highlights the potential of these services to contribute positively to urban sustainability goals.

---

[76] https://www.statista.com/outlook/mmo/shared-mobility/ride-hailing/worldwide

[77] https://www.researchgate.net/publication/373772264_a_study_on_custom ers_satisfaction_towards_uber_eats_online_food_delivery_services_with_speci al_reference_to_coimbatore_city

[78] https://www.sciencedirect.com/science/article/pii/S0191261521000114

The rise of personalized mobility services represents a pivotal cultural shift in transportation preferences. As cities adapt to accommodate these changes, government and private transportation service providers need to understand evolving consumer behaviors. It will drive widespread adoption and be crucial in shaping the future of mobility solutions responsive to metropolitan challenges and sustainable development goals.

Technological Innovations Driving Change

Advancements in technology have been fundamental in reshaping the landscape of transportation. They have been crucial in enhancing its efficiency, safety, and sustainability. Among these advancements are two pivotal technologies—Artificial Intelligence (AI) and the Internet of Things (IoT)—and their transformative impact on metropolitan mobility.

Artificial Intelligence (AI) has emerged as a critical tool in modern transportation systems. It revolutionized how cities manage traffic flow, optimize routes, and enhance efficiency. AI applications in traffic management have reshaped urban mobility by enabling real-time analysis of traffic patterns and predictive modeling to optimize traffic signals and routing.

For instance, cities like Singapore and London have implemented AI-powered traffic management systems that adjust in real-time based on traffic conditions, reducing congestion and improving the flow of vehicles.[79]

Moreover, statistics highlight the tangible benefits of AI in transportation. According to a report on AI traffic systems in Pittsburgh, Pennsylvania, AI-powered traffic management systems can reduce travel times by up to 25%.[80] It further hints toward a potential decrease in fuel consumption and emissions by optimizing traffic flow. These systems analyze vast amounts of data from sensors, cameras, and GPS devices to make informed decisions that improve urban mobility.

The report also indicated a future where ride-sharing companies are moving toward using autonomous vehicles (AVs). An urban public mobility landscape with AVs promises safer and more efficient transportation options. AVs equipped with AI technologies can navigate complex urban environments, interact with pedestrians, and anticipate traffic patterns, reducing accidents and enhancing mobility for all road users.[81]

A notable case study is the deployment of autonomous shuttles in cities like Gothenburg, Sweden.[82] These driverless vehicles operate on designated routes to provide first and last-mile connectivity while significantly reducing

---

[79]https://businessforwardauc.com/2024/06/13/how-ai-is-revolutionizing-road-safety/

[80]https://www.smartcitiesdive.com/news/this-ai-traffic-system-in-pittsburgh-has-reduced-travel-time-by-25/447494/

[81] https://www.mdpi.com/2673-7590/4/3/34

[82]https://www.researchgate.net/publication/347081818_User_acceptance_of_mixed-traffic_autonomous_shuttles_in_Gothenburg_Sweden

traffic congestion and carbon emissions. The integration of AI in AVs represented a transformative shift toward sustainable and intelligent transportation solutions.[83]

IoT and Its Recurring Impact on Mobility

The Internet of Things (IoT) is crucial in transforming mobility. It enables real-time data collection, analysis, and communication across interconnected devices and systems. Cities and counties worldwide are leveraging IoT technologies to enhance public transit operations and improve efficiency.

A great example is Barcelona, which has implemented smart bus stops equipped with sensors that provide real-time information on bus schedules, occupancy levels, and air quality.[84] This data enables commuters to make informed decisions and enhances the reliability of public transit systems.[85]

As mentioned in the previous chapter, IoT can enhance modern transportation systems to reduce travel times, optimize routes, and improve passenger experiences. By integrating IoT sensors into infrastructure and vehicles, smart cities can monitor traffic flow, manage parking availability, and coordinate public transit services more effectively.

---

[83] https://iopscience.iop.org/article/10.1088/1755-1315/588/4/042002
[84] https://www.mdpi.com/2624-6511/3/2/23
[85]https://datasmart.hks.harvard.edu/news/article/how-smart-city-barcelona-brought-the-internet-of-things-to-life-789

A successful case study is the City of Santander in Spain, which has deployed IoT sensors across its transportation network.[86] These sensors monitor traffic conditions, parking availability, and pedestrian movement, providing valuable insights for urban planners to optimize infrastructure and improve mobility.

Integrating AI and IoT in transportation represents a paradigm shift toward smarter, more efficient, and sustainable mobility solutions. By harnessing the power of these technologies, cities and counties can address congestion, enhance safety, and improve the overall quality of life for residents and visitors. More importantly, smart cities can position themselves at the forefront of the future of transportation.

The Integration of Mobility Models and Urban Planning

The synergy between mobility models and urban planning has been pivotal in shaping sustainable and efficient transportation systems. Integrating smart cities, integrated transportation systems, and the role of public-private partnerships has fostered innovation in urban mobility solutions.

Smart cities continue to pioneer comprehensive transportation strategies that integrate various mobility options to enhance connectivity, reduce congestion, and

---

[86]https://www.sciencedirect.com/science/article/abs/pii/S1389128613004337

promote sustainable urban development. Cities like Portland, Oregon, have implemented robust integrated transportation systems prioritizing cycling, public transit, and electric vehicles (EVs).[87] The city's infrastructure supports extensive cycling lanes, efficient transportation networks, and EV charging stations. This has the potential to significantly reduce the dependency on private cars and promote eco-friendly modes of transportation in the upcoming years.

Statistics underscore the benefits of integrated transportation systems. A comprehensive American Public Transportation Association study shows numerous US cities have well-developed public transit networks.[88] As a result of it, these cities are experiencing lower congestion levels and reduced greenhouse gas emissions.

Furthermore, some cities like Portland, Oregon, have also witnessed a nearly 10% reduction in fuel consumption thanks to TriMet, a commuter rail service for the public. These cities have significantly reduced traffic congestion and air pollution by promoting multimodal transportation options.

Moreover, integrated transportation systems improve accessibility and mobility for everyone. Consequently, this contributes to social inclusion, equity, and economic growth.

---

[87]https://www.portland.gov/sites/default/files/2021/2030-bicycle-plan-progress-report_final_1.pdf
[88]https://www.apta.com/wpcontent/uploads/Resources/resources/reportsand publications/Documents/greenhouse_brochure.pdf

By connecting metropolitan areas with employment hubs and cultural centers, cities can enhance quality of life and foster inclusive urban environments.

Public-Private Partnerships in Transportation

Public-private partnerships (PPPs) have also played a critical role in enhancing transportation infrastructure and service delivery by leveraging private sector expertise and resources. The partnership between Transport for London (TfL) and ride-sharing platforms is a compelling case study.[89] Through collaborative efforts, TfL integrates ride-sharing services into its public transit network, providing commuters with seamless first- and last-mile connectivity.[90] This partnership improves passenger experience, reduces congestion, and supports sustainable urban mobility goals.

Reports highlight the economic impacts of PPPs in transportation. According to a report by the World Economic Forum, every dollar invested in public transportation infrastructure through PPPs generates multiple economic benefits, including job creation, increased productivity, and enhanced regional connectivity.[91] These partnerships facilitate innovative financing models that reduce public expenditure while improving service quality and efficiency.[92]

---

[89]https://www.cnbc.com/2018/12/11/uber-reportedly-wants-to-offer-london-bus-and-tube-data-in-its-app.html

[90]https://www.sciencedirect.com/science/article/abs/pii/S2213624X19300045

[91]https://www3.weforum.org/docs/AF13/WEF_AF13_Strategic_Infrastructure_Initiative.pdf

[92]https://www.weforum.org/agenda/2021/04/here-s-why-cities-should-invest-in-public-transport/

Furthermore, PPPs contribute to technological advancements in transportation, such as autonomous vehicles and smart infrastructure. Companies like May Mobility, Waymo, and Tesla collaborate with municipalities to pilot AVs and deploy IoT-enabled traffic management systems.[93] This paves the way for safer and more efficient mobility solutions.

Integrating innovative mobility models and urban planning through smart cities and public-private partnerships can prove highly beneficial in the shift to more sustainable and inclusive transportation systems. However, this requires two-way collaboration to fuel rapid innovation, which can address smart cities' evolving urban mobility challenges. As a result, it will improve environmental sustainability and overall quality of life for residents and visitors alike.

Visionary Outlook on the Future of Mobility

As we look ahead, the future of mobility holds promising prospects driven by sustainability-driven innovation and transformative technologies. The shift toward sustainable transportation solutions, especially electric vehicles (EVs) and renewable energy sources, is pivotal in reducing carbon emissions and mitigating environmental impact.[94]

---

[93] https://www.mdpi.com/1424-8220/23/4/1963

[94] https://www.researchgate.net/publication/378907620_Transforming_the_t ransportation_sector_Mitigating_greenhouse_gas_emissions_through_electric_ vehicles_EVs_and_exploring_sustainable_pathways

Globally, there has been a significant uptake in electric vehicles, supported by governmental incentives and advancements in battery technology. According to the *Global EV Outlook 2023: Accelerating the transition to electric mobility*. International Energy Agency, the IEA highlights how the uptake of electric vehicles has continued to accelerate globally, with a record number of EVs on the road in 2023. The report provides insights into the growth trends, governmental policies, and technological advancements driving electric vehicle adoption.[95]

According to the International Energy Agency (IEA), the global electric car stock exceeded 10 million in 2020. It marked a substantial milestone in the transition toward cleaner mobility options.

Cities like Seattle and Washington have emerged as frontrunners in promoting electric mobility through robust infrastructure development and incentivizing EV adoption among residents.[96] Oslo's comprehensive approach includes extensive charging networks and EV charger rebates. This has positioned the city as a sustainable mobility leader in Europe.

Singapore's implementation of shared electric scooter services has enhanced first and last-mile connectivity for

---

[95]https://www.iea.org/reports/global-ev-outlook-2021/trends-and-developments-in-electric-vehicle-markets
[96] https://seattle.gov/city-light/energy/electrification/transportation-electrification/multifamily-ev-charging

commuters.[97] It reduces reliance on private cars and promotes sustainable urban mobility. Similarly, Portland, Oregon, has embraced bike-sharing initiatives that provide residents with affordable and environmentally friendly transportation options that complement existing public transit systems.

Furthermore, advancements in autonomous vehicles (AVs) and smart infrastructure are poised to redefine mobility experiences in metropolitan environments. Companies like May Mobility, Waymo, and Cruise are piloting AV technologies that promise safer, more efficient transportation solutions by leveraging AI and real-time data analytics.[98] These innovations improve traffic management and enhance mobility accessibility for elderly and disabled populations. Moreover, they foster more inclusive and equitable metropolitan communities.

As we conclude this chapter on the transformative shifts reshaping the future of mobility, it's clear that the road ahead is paved with immense potential and challenges. The emphasis on technology, sustainability, and personalized solutions has set a strong foundation for passenger transportation. However, while technological advancements and innovative models are essential, the human aspect remains a crucial element that cannot be overlooked.

---

[97]https://www.researchgate.net/publication/350268828_E-scooter_sharing_to_serve_short-distance_transit_trips_A_Singapore_case

[98]https://www.forbes.com/sites/bradtempleton/2023/02/28/waymo-and-cruise-have-both-hit-1m-miles-with-no-driver-but-waymo-published-detailed-safety-data/

In the next chapter, we focus on *The Human Element in Mobility*. Here, we will explore individuals, communities, and societal behaviors' profound impact on shaping transportation systems. We will delve into how human-centric design, inclusivity, and equitable access influence the future of mobility, making it smarter and more efficient, compassionate, and responsive to the needs of all. Prepare to uncover people's role in crafting a future where technology and humanity move together, hand in hand.

Chapter 9
The Human Element in Mobility: Why People-Centric Solutions Drive Lasting Change

"The ultimate driving machine is one powered by the mind and driven by the heart."

-Elon Musk

The mobility industry has been evolving continuously. It is driven by technological advancements, changing societal needs, and cultural shifts. The broad mobility industry has transformed into a dynamic ecosystem deeply linked to human experiences and aspirations. Empathy and user-centric innovations are reshaping the future of mobility design, placing human needs and preferences at the forefront of transportation evolution.

The focus has expanded beyond efficiency and functionality to encompass mobility's emotional and practical aspects. Today, vehicles are no longer just modes of transportation. Instead, they have become personalized environments catering to individual preferences, enhancing comfort, and fostering connectivity. This transformation is mainly due to visionary concepts and groundbreaking technologies that promise to revolutionize how we interact with transportation in the future.

Understanding the importance of empathetic design and user-centric innovations will help us uncover these elements' pivotal role in improving the quality of transportation services and shaping a more inclusive and sustainable mobility landscape. We will examine critical case studies and emerging trends. Moreover, we will highlight how empathy is becoming a driving force behind the next generation of vehicles and mobility solutions.

Examining the Role of Empathy in Mobility Design

Concept cars represent more than just prototypes of future vehicles. They have been developed on a framework of empathetic design for customers in the automotive industry. Moreover, these visionary platforms serve as testbeds for groundbreaking technologies and design philosophies aimed at enhancing the human experience of mobility.[99]

Companies like Toyota, BMW, Volvo, Ford, and Lincoln are leaders in integrating empathy into their concept cars. These companies have set new standards for the industry. With its LQ concept car, Toyota showcased a combination of technology and emotion in automotive design.[100] It was equipped with an AI-powered assistant named "Yui," the LQ adapts its interior environment based on passengers' moods.[101]

Furthermore, it employed features like adjustable lighting, aroma, and climate control. This enhanced comfort

---

[99]https://dspace5.zcu.cz/bitstream/11025/37399/1/Chotovinsky_Doctoral_T hesis_180403.pdf

[100] https://global.toyota/en/newsroom/corporate/30063126.html

[101] https://www.dezeen.com/2019/10/17/toyota-lq-concept-car/

and fostered a deeper connection between vehicle and occupants, transforming the driving experience into a personalized journey of relaxation and safety.[102]

BMW's Vision Next 100 concept car also took empathetic mobility design to another level with its shape-shifting capabilities and adaptive interiors. The car's flexible outer skin adjusts aerodynamically, and the interior dynamically reconfigures based on driving modes. This ensures optimal comfort and engagement for passengers.[103]

This visionary approach observes personalized mobility design in a future where vehicles intuitively respond to individual needs, preferences, and driving conditions. On the other hand, Volvo's 360c concept car explored the boundaries of autonomous and electric travel, focusing on versatility and inclusivity.[104] It features a modular interior that can transform into a mobile office, living space, or entertainment lounge to cater to diverse passenger needs.

The adaptive design was developed to highlight Volvo's commitment to human-centric mobility. However, it also helped the company share a vision of the future where travel becomes an integrated part of daily life to improve both productivity and relaxation on the move. [105] Similarly, Ford's

---

[102]https://www.researchgate.net/publication/378291359_Case_Study_Analysis_of_Toyota_Company_and_make_time_to_market

[103] https://www.wired.com/story/bmw-vision-next-100-pictures/

[104]https://www.media.volvocars.com/global/en-gb/media/pressreleases/237020/volvo-cars-new-360c-autonomous-concept-reimagining-the-work-life-balance-and-the-future-of-cities

[105] https://www.forbes.com/sites/nargessbanks/2018/10/22/volvo-driverless-360c-car/

exploration of electric vehicle innovations through its Team Edison initiative emphasizes responsive materials and smart technologies. [106] [107]

These advancements were aimed to tailor the vehicle's ambiance and functionality to align with the driver's mood and preferences. They promised a more intuitive and enjoyable driving experience. The main concepts like changeable exterior colors showed Ford's vision of vehicles as dynamic assistants that could seamlessly adapt to individual lifestyles and emotions. [108]

On the other hand, the Lincoln's Star concept car epitomized luxury electric mobility with its "coast-to-coast" dashboard display and customizable interface. [109] It was designed to provide a comfortable environment on wheels. [110] [111]

The car adjusted the lighting, sound, and scent to create a serene environment, showing how Lincoln focused on empathetic mobility designs for its futuristic automotive projects. [112]

---

[106] https://www.forbes.com/sites/dalebuss/2017/10/02/ford-creates-team-edison-to-accelerate-its-efforts-in-battery-electric-vehicles/

[107] https://www.sciencedirect.com/topics/engineering/electric-vehicle-initiative

[108] https://www.reuters.com/article/technology/ford-creates-team-to-ramp-up-electric-vehicle-development-idUSKCN1C726X/

[109] https://www.lincoln.com/concept-future/

[110] https://www.topgear.com/car-news/concept/lincoln-star-concept-has-custom-storage-your-slippers

[111] https://cal.msu.edu/news/msu-education-helping-drive-work-on-all-electric-lincoln-star-concept-car/

[112] https://www.forbes.com/sites/kyleedward/2022/10/05/lincoln-star-concept-previews-the-brands-electric-future/

These companies' concept cars served as the groundwork for empathy-driven innovation in mobility.[113] By pushing boundaries and reimagining the relationship between vehicles and passengers, Toyota, BMW, Volvo, Ford, and Lincoln started paving the way for a future where transportation was a more seamless extension of human lifestyles and emotions.

Toyota LQ Concept Car

The Toyota LQ concept car represented a shift in automotive design by integrating advanced AI technologies to enhance passenger comfort and safety. This innovation had an AI-powered assistant named "Yui," which responded to commands and proactively anticipated passengers' needs and emotions. This groundbreaking approach transformed the driving experience and set new emotional connectivity and vehicle safety standards.

Yui, the AI companion within the Toyota LQ, appeared as a bridge between technology and human interaction. It had sophisticated sensors and cameras to monitor passengers' facial expressions, body language, and vocal cues to gauge their emotional state. Interpreting these signals adjusts the car's interior environment in real-time.

For instance, if it detected signs of stress or fatigue, it would activate soothing lighting, adjust the cabin temperature, or play calming music to enhance relaxation and well-being. Moreover, it had capabilities beyond

---

[113] https://www.businessinsider.com/lincoln-ford-electric-car-concept-star-2022-4

promising comfort and real-time adjustments for customers. The AI assistant could engage passengers in natural conversations to provide personalized recommendations for entertainment, navigation, and even local points of interest.

This interactive feature was aimed to enhance the overall journey experience and build a sense of companionship and emotional engagement between the driver and the AI companion. It transformed the car into a supportive environment rather than just a mode of transportation. Since emotional connectivity was at the core of Toyota's vision for the LQ concept car, the company created a vehicle that adapts to passengers' emotional states and preferences.

Toyota aimed to strengthen the bond between humans and machines through a proactive approach to enhance passenger comfort while promoting safer driving environments.

For instance, Yui's ability to monitor and respond to emotional cues reduced driver distraction and stress. As a result, it improved overall road safety. Furthermore, it preemptively addressed potential sources of discomfort or tension, such as traffic congestion or adverse weather conditions. It could maintain a focused and relaxed driving atmosphere. This helped the drivers remain alert and responsive for a safer and more enjoyable journey.

BMW Vision Next 100

The BMW Vision Next 100 concept car was another pioneering attempt at empathetic automotive design. It focused on emphasizing dynamic adaptability and personalized experiences. It had futuristic shape-shifting features and adaptive interiors. That was because BMW aimed to redefine driving by integrating cutting-edge technologies that respond intuitively to drivers' needs and preferences.

The BMW Vision Next 100's innovation was its shape-shifting architecture. It dynamically adjusted its external dimensions to optimize aerodynamics and efficiency based on driving conditions. This adaptive capability enhanced performance significantly. In addition, it has reduced energy consumption and environmental impact.

Inside the BMW Vision Next 100 cabin, the company introduced the concept of adaptive interiors that also changed according to the driving mode and passenger preferences. For example, during autonomous driving, the steering wheel retracted seamlessly into the dashboard, creating a more spacious and lounge-like environment for passengers. In the same way, the interior configuration was adjusted to prioritize driver engagement and control in manual mode. It emphasized ergonomic design and intuitive interface layouts.

The BMW concept car was a glimpse into a future where driving experiences were personalized and integrated with everyday life, much like other leading companies, including Volvo and Toyota. The car was built on advanced AI and sensor technology to adapt to individual driving styles. Moreover, it also allowed the AI-powered car to anticipate user preferences through predictive analytics and machine learning algorithms.

For instance, the adaptive interiors learned from previous driving patterns and environmental conditions to automatically adjust seating positions, climate settings, and entertainment options. This level of personalization significantly improved comfort and convenience for drivers. The shape-shifting features extended beyond aesthetics. They were designed to redefine the relationship between vehicles and their users.

Volvo 360c

The Volvo 360c concept car was a bold exploration into the future of autonomous and versatile transportation solutions. It also had a similar emphasis on inclusivity and adaptability for drivers. This visionary concept challenged conventional notions of mobility by changing the interior space as a multifunctional environment for diverse passenger needs and preferences.

Volvo's innovation was the autonomous capability of the 360c, which saved passengers from dealing with traditional driving responsibilities. This autonomy enabled the vehicle to operate seamlessly within urban and intercity environments. This was possible through the integration of sophisticated sensor technologies and AI-driven navigation systems as well. More importantly, these technologies prioritize safe and efficient travel.

The company built a versatile interior layout with ergonomic and unconventional seating arrangements. It also featured a modular seating configuration that could transform into various setups like a mobile office or relaxation lounge-type environment. It could even transform into a sleeping compartment due to autonomous driving technology.

This adaptability enhanced passenger comfort during extended journeys and accommodated diverse mobility needs. This included individuals with disabilities or specific medical requirements. The concept car was a widely reviewed and highly appraised initiative by Volvo. It was developed for inclusive mobility solutions, prioritizing accessibility and convenience for all passengers. Volvo aimed to revolutionize personal transportation with autonomous technology and versatile interior designs.

Moreover, it represented a shift toward sustainable urban mobility and the potential for reduced congestion and emissions through efficient autonomous driving capabilities. This sustainable approach aligned with Volvo's broader vision of creating cities where transportation was efficient and improved the quality of life for residents through shared mobility and reduced environmental impact.

Ford's Vision for Electric Mobility

Ford ventured into electric mobility to combine responsive materials and advanced smart technologies to redefine the future of personal transportation. The company decided to start initiatives that could improve EV efficiency and enhance the mobility experience through intuitive design and sustainable practices. Ford planned to integrate responsive materials and smart technologies within its vehicle lineup.

Initially, the innovations were engineered to optimize energy consumption, but later, they were focused on enhancing vehicle performance and improving user convenience. For instance, Ford researched and developed lightweight materials to improve battery efficiency without compromising safety or durability.

Similarly, smart technologies like predictive analytics and artificial intelligence (AI) further augmented the driving experience by anticipating driver behavior and optimizing vehicle functions accordingly. These leading automotive companies followed suit when merging smart technologies for empathetic mobility designs and improving driver convenience.

The company showcased its commitment to developing interconnected ecosystems integrating EVs with smart city infrastructure and digital platforms. This would require leveraging data-driven insights and collaborative partnerships to empower users with unprecedented control over their mobility choices while minimizing environmental impact.

It also planned to initiate projects to expand charging infrastructure and promote sustainable manufacturing practices. The company's ultimate goal was to foster electric vehicle adoption through accessible pricing and leasing options.

User-Centric Mobility Designs for Enhanced Accessibility and Personalization

Ride-sharing services were also pivotal players in improving the personal mobility landscape. They transformed how people commute and made transportation more inclusive and accessible for the users.

The foremost ride-sharing giants have implemented comprehensive initiatives to ensure their services cater to a diverse range of passengers, including those with disabilities.[114] These initiatives can help to make ride-sharing facilities more inclusive and convenient.

One prominent initiative was the "Uber Access" program, which offers wheelchair-accessible vehicles (WAVs) equipped with ramps or lifts, enabling passengers with mobility challenges to travel more independently and comfortably.[115] This program carries the potential to bridge the accessibility gap in urban transportation to provide reliable options for users who require specialized accommodations. Similarly, Lyft adopted a collaborative approach to improving accessibility within its ride-sharing services. The company partnered with third-party providers to integrate wheelchair-accessible vehicles into its fleet

---

[114]https://www.theverge.com/23199117/ride-sharing-disabled-passengers-accessibility-uber-lyft

[115] https://www.uber.com/en-GB/blog/uber-access-and-assist/

through the "Lyft WAV" program.[116] This collaboration expanded the availability of accessible transportation options to passengers and offered greater flexibility and choice when planning their journeys.

This inclusive approach not only enhanced accessibility but also built a sense of community and partnership among stakeholders committed to improving mobility for all commuters.

The impact of Uber and Lyft's initiatives extends beyond the provision of accessible vehicles. These programs were a significant step toward creating a more equitable transportation ecosystem where convenient urban mobility was accessible to individuals of all abilities.

The Impact of Integrative Mobility Apps

Integrating various transportation modes into cohesive and user-friendly platforms revolutionized how individuals navigate in urban centers worldwide, mainly in smart cities. The leading innovators in this space were Citymapper and Moovit.[117]

The two innovative applications redefined urban mobility by consolidating diverse transportation options into streamlined

---

[116]https://www.lyft.com/blog/posts/wheelchair-accessible-vehicles-rent-rideshare-lyft

[117]https://www.researchgate.net/publication/346283222_Datainfrastructure _in_the_smart_city_Understanding_the_infrastructural_power_of_Citymapper _app_through_technicity_of_data

and personalized journey-planning tools.[118] Citymapper and Moovit leveraged advanced technologies to aggregate real-time data from multiple transportation sources.[119] These included buses, trains, subways, rideshares, and even micro-mobility options like bikes and scooters.

This integration helped users to access comprehensive and up-to-the-minute information on routes, schedules, and travel times.[120] Furthermore, it helped them to make informed decisions about their journeys. This was possible through a unified platform that combined disparate transit systems into apps that simplified the complexity of urban travel. As a result, users had their hands on a more seamless experience from planning to execution.[121]

The ability to extract real-time data for reliable and efficient mobility planning as part of urban transportation was central to the success of Citymapper and Moovit. The real-time updates on traffic conditions, service disruptions, and route changes allowed users to adapt their travel plans dynamically. This minimized delays and optimized transit choices.

---

[118]https://assets.publishing.service.gov.uk/media/5dcd8417ed915d071ca23 9e9/future-of-mobility-strategy.pdf

[119]https://data.europa.eu/en/news-events/news/moovit-global-transport-application

[120]https://ridewithvia.com/news/citymapper-the-ultimate-journey-planning-app-unlocks-features-that-make-it-easier-to-prioritize-safety-convenience-and-speed-on-every-trip

[121]https://www.gov.uk/government/publications/mobility-as-a-service-maas-code-of-practice/mobility-as-a-service-code-of-practice

This responsiveness potentially improved the overall travel experience and reduced congestion and environmental impact by encouraging more efficient use of transportation resources. Citymapper and Moovit helped commuters personalize their journeys by responsibly using insights into user preferences, historical travel data, and predictive analytics.

These apps generate tailored route recommendations that consider factors such as preferred modes of transport, accessibility needs, and desired arrival times. More importantly, this customization optimizes every journey according to individual preferences and circumstances to achieve higher commuter satisfaction.

Observing Futuristic Personal Mobility Concepts

Advancements in autonomous vehicle technology are one of the main drivers behind the transformation in the personal mobility space. May Mobility, Waymo, and Tesla are leading this revolution and offering innovations that promise to redefine how individuals commute and travel.

Autonomous vehicles (AVs) are a clear shift in transportation. They offer safer, more efficient, and accessible mobility solutions for commuters from all socio-economic backgrounds and needs. These vehicles operate on a combination of sensors, cameras, radar, and advanced AI algorithms to navigate roads autonomously. And that reduces the need for human intervention.

When calculated, this reduces the potential for human error as AVs can significantly reduce traffic accidents and fatalities, making roads safer for all of us. AVs also show promising results in optimizing traffic flow and reducing congestion. Through coordinated communication and precise control over acceleration and braking, autonomous systems can mitigate the inefficiencies caused by human drivers. This can lead to smoother traffic patterns and shorter commute times.

Waymo, a subsidiary of Alphabet Inc., has emerged as a leader in AV technology. The company conducted extensive testing and deployment initiatives across various regions.[122] Their fleet of self-driving cars accumulated millions of miles on public roads. This helped them refine their algorithms and safety protocols to achieve high levels of reliability.

Similarly, Tesla's Autopilot feature integrates semi-autonomous driving capabilities into their electric vehicles. [123] It was perceived as a pioneering innovation because it showed a future where vehicles could be safely handed full autonomy over travel. The company's iterative approach to software updates and data-driven improvements helped advance its novel AV technology while ensuring safety and regulatory compliance.

On the other hand, May Mobility's Multi-Policy Decision Making (MPDM) system reframes the challenge for AVs.

---

[122]https://www.researchgate.net/publication/374246602_Modeling_Waymo 's_Shared_Autonomous_Vehicle_Service_in_Phoenix_Using_e3value
[123]https://www.irjet.net/archives/V3/i9/IRJET-V3I969.pdf

Rather than telling a vehicle what to do and when—which is what rules-based systems do—MPDM continually runs real-time, on-board simulations to imagine thousands of possible scenarios every second virtually, enabling a vehicle to decide which action is the safest.

The company's innovative approach significantly lowers implementation costs and deployment, bringing a flexible approach to multiple operating environments in the AV industry.

Beyond May Mobility, Waymo, and Tesla, traditional automakers such as Toyota, General Motors, and Ford invest heavily in AV research and development.[124]

The widespread adoption of autonomous vehicles will hinge on overcoming technical, regulatory, and societal challenges. As AV technology matures, policymakers and metropolitan planners must collaborate and establish clear guidelines for deployment and integration into existing transportation infrastructure.

Public acceptance and trust in autonomous systems will also play an essential role in shaping the future of personal mobility.[125] AVs will be a significant development in personal mobility in the coming years.[126] With the potential to redefine how people commute and travel, it will also

---

[124]https://www.cnbc.com/2022/11/13/ford-vs-gm-same-industry-two-increasingly-different-companies.html

[125]https://www.sciencedirect.com/science/article/abs/pii/S2214140523001627

[126]https://www.mckinsey.com/industries/automotive-and-assembly/our-insights/autonomous-drivings-future-convenient-and-connected

supplement continued innovation and collaboration across industry sectors.

Paving the Way for Personalized Travel Experiences Through Technology

The advancements in AI and Machine Learning (ML) are also revolutionary principles in the relationship between commuters and public mobility solutions in urban centers. These technologies have equipped mobility services providers with the tools and algorithmic framework to tailor experiences based on personal preferences. Moreover, they have been influential in enhancing comfort, convenience, and overall satisfaction for passengers.

AI and ML algorithms analyze vast amounts of data, including user preferences, travel patterns, and environmental factors. The goal of this data processing activity is to optimize travel experiences in real time.

AI-powered virtual assistants embedded in vehicles can personalize passenger interactions, ranging from customized recommendations for entertainment and interior climate control settings to preferred destinations. The AI and ML models learn from every interaction with passengers to continuously refine their understanding of user preferences. This has helped in creating more intuitive and responsive travel experiences.

The widespread integration of AI and ML technologies in not just ride-sharing companies but also public transportation and mass transit facilities has profound implications for the future of mobility. AVs with AI-driven navigation systems can adapt to changing road conditions and passenger preferences in real-time, offering seamless and efficient transportation solutions.

AI-powered mobility platforms also have the potential to orchestrate multi-modal journeys. They can integrate public transit and ride-sharing services with personal vehicles to form cohesive travel experiences. Optimized route planning and scheduling also help these platforms reduce travel times while enhancing accessibility for users of diverse mobility needs.

The passenger transportation sector has a unique opportunity to leverage technology to create a highly personalized consumer experience. However, technology alone will not produce this fundamental change.

Providers must embrace hospitality concepts and apply them to their operations with technology as the center of this pivotal change.

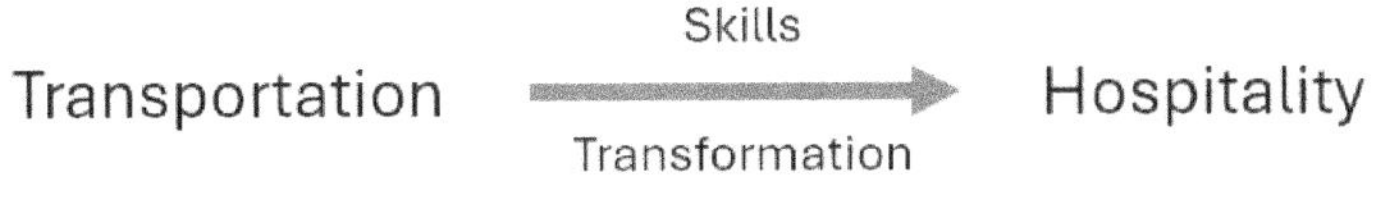

Transportation   →   Hospitality

Skills Transformation

Concepts like The Ritz-Carlton's personalization strategy revolve around creating deeply customized experiences for each guest by anticipating and addressing their needs, even before they express them. Their approach integrates technology, data management, and a unique service philosophy to ensure guests feel valued, engaged, and part of the brand.

A key feature of Ritz-Carlton's personalization is using a cloud-based data system that records guest preferences and behaviors.[127] This system allows staff to tailor each guest's experience based on previous interactions—for example, surprising a guest's child with a personalized cake and greeting upon arrival on her birthday, fostering lifelong loyalty through thoughtful gestures.[128]

The company also empowers employees to provide exceptional service. Each staff member can spend up to $2,000 per guest daily to resolve issues or create delightful experiences without managerial approval.[129] This level of trust enables employees to act quickly and meaningfully, enhancing the guest experience. [130]

Ritz-Carlton's philosophy goes beyond just service—cultivating a culture of belonging. Employees are encouraged to engage meaningfully with guests, demonstrated through stories like retrieving a child's forgotten toy and creating a photo album of the toy's "extended vacation" to ease the child's worries. These

---

[127] https://thebrandhopper.com/2023/09/16/marketing-strategies-and-marketing-mix-of-ritz-carlton/

[128] https://crm.org/articles/ritz-carlton-gold-standards

[129]https://customerthink.com/3_keys_to_customer_service_training_and_re tention_from_ritz_carlton_vp_diana_oreck/#google_vignette

[130] https://thestrategystory.com/2021/06/09/ritz-carlton-business-strategy/

thoughtful actions illustrate the brand's commitment to exceeding expectations at every touchpoint.[131]

Ritz-Carlton sets a high standard for personalized customer service in the hospitality industry through its integrated use of data, empowered staff, and emotional connections.

Furthermore, embracing the Disney way, where they create an exceptional customer experience through personalization, process optimization, and emotional engagement, ensuring that guests feel immersed in "magic" from the moment they interact with the brand. This approach extends across Disney's theme parks, movies, merchandise, and digital platforms.

At the heart of Disney's customer experience are the "Four Keys" principles: **Safety, Courtesy, Show, and Efficiency**.[132] These principles guide Disney's employees, known as "Cast Members," in every interaction.[133] Employees are empowered to exceed expectations, creating delightful moments—personalized greetings, surprise gifts, or swift issue resolution—to enhance guest satisfaction and build emotional connections.[134] For example, suppose a child is disappointed by not meeting the height requirement for a ride. The staff can offer a pass to skip the line at another

---

[131]https://hospitalityinsights.ehl.edu/personalizing-customer-journey

[132] https://disneyinsights.com/disneys-four-keys-to-a-great-guest-experience/

[133] https://www.helpscout.com/blog/disney-customer-experience/

[134] https://www.qualtrics.com/blog/6-ways-disney-world-delivers-top-customer-experiences/

attraction to turn the situation around. (Qualtrics, Disney Insights, etc.)

Disney also leverages technology like the **My Disney Experience app** and **MagicBands**, providing guests seamless access to rides, reservations, and personalized surprises. These innovations improve convenience and create a feeling of exclusivity and personalization for every visitor.[135]

In addition to crafting experiences in physical spaces, Disney integrates its brand across multiple channels—such as movies, streaming services, merchandise, and parks—ensuring that the "magic" continues after guests leave the park. This multi-channel strategy strengthens customer engagement and drives repeat visits, with Disney enjoying a return rate of over 70% from first-time park visitors. (Fabrik Brands)[136]

Through meticulous attention to detail, employee empowerment, and advanced personalization, Disney ensures every guest encounter is memorable, fostering long-term loyalty and making Disney's approach a benchmark in the entertainment industry.

As we learned, transforming organizational skills and intensively using technology throughout the provider

---

[135] https://www.latterly.org/disney-marketing-strategy/
[136] Fabrik Brands. (n.d.). *Disney marketing strategy: The secrets behind the magic*. Fabrik Brands. Retrieved November 28, 2024, from https://fabrikbrands.com

process is fundamental to embracing Personalized Travel Experiences.

The human element in mobility has shown us that empathy, inclusivity, and user-centric designs are critical in shaping how we experience transportation today. The importance of creating connections that go beyond utility to foster comfort, accessibility, and personalization cannot be understated. Yet, the tools enabling this human-centric evolution are themselves worth exploring further. The future of transportation hinges not just on understanding human needs but on how we leverage technology and innovation to meet those needs.

In the next chapter, *Technology and Innovation*, we will delve deeper into the advanced technologies redefining mobility. From AI-driven solutions to IoT integrations and land or aerial autonomous vehicles, these innovations are not just future concepts—they are the building blocks of present and upcoming mobility systems. These advancements will pave the way for hyper-accelerated growth, pushing the boundaries of what is possible and propelling the mobility industry into an era of smarter and more connected transportation. Prepare to discover how these technological breakthroughs will revolutionize how we move and interact with the world around us.

Chapter 10
Technology and Innovation: How Breakthroughs Are Shaping the Future of Mobility

"Innovation distinguishes between a leader and a follower."

- Steve Jobs

The rapid technological advancement has played an instrumental role in the future of mobility, primarily through innovations that have surpassed expectations. We have begun transitioning from traditional modes of transportation to more advanced systems where technology is the powerhouse of modern mobility.

It has begun influencing how we conceive, experience, and manage mobility. From autonomous vehicles that promise to redefine road safety to integrated transportation networks that blend ground and air travel, the landscape of mobility is evolving at an unprecedented pace.

This chapter will discuss the critical aspects of this technological revolution and focus on how electrification, autonomous vehicles, personalization, and integrated transportation systems catalyze change to hyper-exponential growth in the new Post-Digital Econnomy. We will explore the significant impact of 5G and Low Earth Orbit (LEO) satellite communications in enhancing connectivity and operational efficiency. At the same time, we will also examine the role of artificial intelligence (AI) in revolutionizing mobility services under the following future premise,

THE FUTURE OF MOBILITY WILL BE ELECTRIC, AUTONOMOUS, PERSONALIZED AND CONNECTED

The rapid convergence of these six technology elements (Electric, Autonomous, AI, Land/Air, Personalization, and Communication) will contribute to a more connected and efficient transportation ecosystem and set the stage for a future where mobility is smarter, safer, and more personalized. There will be real-world case studies similar to the ones we have been analyzing regarding the changes in the technological landscape and environmental goals of the modern mobility industry.

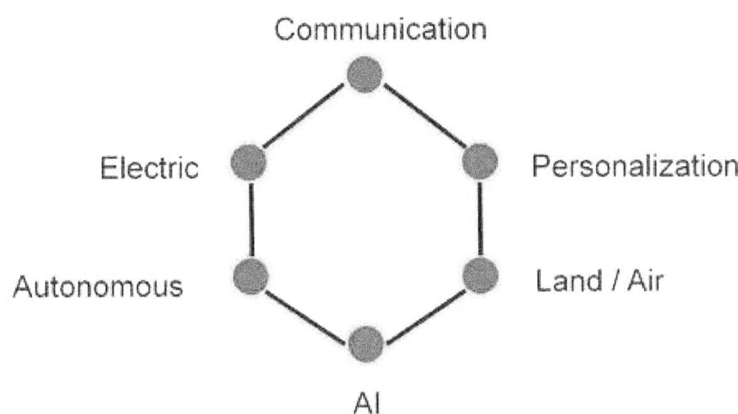

The Drive Toward the Future of Mobility with Autonomous Vehicles

The field of autonomous vehicles (AVs) has been seeing rapid technological advancements. Moreover, countless global initiatives have been supported and driven by the leading automobile players in the global industry.

As discussed in earlier chapters, companies like May Mobility, Waymo, and Tesla continue to push the boundaries of what is possible in the AV markets. They have been challenging issues related to deployment and regulation. Furthermore, a significant move toward improving public perception has helped the companies in their initiatives. Their ongoing efforts to address the current challenges will play a crucial role in determining the potential trajectory of AVs.

Case Study of May Mobility Autonomous Vehicles

May Mobility was founded in 2017 and is based in Ann Arbor, Michigan. It is transforming urban transportation with its autonomous electric shuttles. These shuttles have advanced sensors like LiDAR, proprietary multi-policy decision-making sensors, cameras, and radar. They offer a safe, efficient, and eco-friendly alternative to traditional transit systems.

These sensors are part of the advanced perception system that enables their autonomous shuttles to detect and classify objects around the vehicle. The system also combines data from various sources like LiDAR, cameras, and radar to create a comprehensive 360-degree view of the surroundings.

This proprietary technology is highly suitable for increasing the efficiency and accuracy of autonomous vehicles' decision-making capabilities. It becomes increasingly important in diverse and dynamic urban environments, further bolstering the safety and efficiency of the company's shuttles.

These vehicles operate on flexible, fixed routes in city centers, corporate campuses, and universities. As a result, they complement the existing public transportation by providing convenient first-mile/last-mile mobility solutions.

Key partnerships with municipalities and companies like Toyota have also been crucial in integrating these vehicles into urban environments. May Mobility's vehicles potentially reduce emissions and noise pollution while improving all transportation access. This also includes underserved communities to enhance economic opportunities and quality of life.

Looking ahead, May Mobility plans to expand its fleet and enter new markets through continuous innovations in AI and vehicle-to-infrastructure communication. Moreover, the company aims to enhance the safety and accessibility features of its fleet to incorporate more communities and population segments.

Case Study of Waymo's Autonomous Vehicles

Waymo, a subsidiary of Alphabet Inc., has pioneered AV technology. Its development center is in Phoenix, Arizona, where the company has conducted extensive pilot programs. These trials, part of Waymo's broader strategy to integrate self-driving technology into everyday transportation, have showcased the potential for autonomous vehicles to transform urban mobility.

Waymo's vehicles, equipped with advanced LiDAR systems, cameras, and machine learning algorithms, have demonstrated significant improvements in road safety. According to a 2023 report by Waymo, their autonomous fleet has covered over 20 million miles in autonomous mode, contributing to a noticeable reduction in traffic incidents in their test areas.[137] This technology enhances safety by reducing human error and promises to improve traffic flow and reduce congestion.

Case Study of Tesla's Full Self-Driving (FSD) Capabilities

Tesla's approach to autonomous driving is embodied in its Full Self-Driving (FSD) capabilities, an advanced version of its Autopilot system. Tesla's FSD includes Navigate on Autopilot, Auto Lane Change, and Traffic Light Control features.[138] Recent updates have focused on improving the

---

[137]https://downloads.ctfassets.net/sv23gofxcuiz/4gZ7ZUxd4SRj1D1W6z3r
pR/2ea16814cdb42f9e8eb34cae4f30b35d/2021-03-waymo-safety-report.pdf
[138] https://www.tesla.com/support/autopilot

system's ability to handle complex driving scenarios like navigating through city intersections and responding to dynamic road conditions.[139]

The real-world performance of Tesla's FSD has been intensely scrutinized,[140] drawing both acclaim and criticism from users and industry experts alike. User feedback reveals a mixed picture: while many appreciate the convenience, seamless navigation, and impressive advanced features that enhance daily commutes, others have raised legitimate concerns about the system's reliability and safety in specific driving conditions.[141] These include complex urban environments, unpredictable weather, and sudden pedestrian crossings.

Despite these challenges, Tesla remains undeterred, continuously refining its technology to enhance safety protocols, situational awareness, and response times. This relentless pursuit of improvement is evident with the launch of its new *Robotaxi* service. The Robotaxi represents Tesla's ambitious leap toward providing fully autonomous ride-hailing solutions, bringing the company closer to realizing its vision of a highly automated transportation ecosystem.

The Robotaxi is engineered to leverage Tesla's latest FSD updates, integrating enhanced AI algorithms, upgraded sensor arrays, and more responsive real-time data processing.

---

[139]https://www.tesla.com/ownersmanual/modely/en_us/GUID-2CB60804-9CEA-4F4B-8B04-09B991368DC5.html

[140] https://www.ncbi.nlm.nih.gov/pmc/articles/PMC9996345/

[141]https://www.bloomberg.com/graphics/2023-tesla-survey/autopilot-features-satisfaction/

These advancements aim to overcome the system's limitations and broaden its applicability across diverse road networks and traffic conditions. Tesla's Robotaxi showcases its commitment to pushing the boundaries of autonomous driving. Also, it hints at a future where personal and shared mobility solutions are more accessible, efficient, and seamlessly integrated into urban transit systems.

As Tesla refines its FSD technology with each iteration, the Robotaxi marks a significant milestone. It is designed to adapt, learn, and improve, potentially setting a new standard for autonomous vehicle performance and safety.

Rising Global Initiatives and Challenges for Autonomous Mobility

China is aggressively advancing autonomous mobility through several high-profile initiatives. Baidu's Apollo project is a significant example that aims to create a comprehensive autonomous driving ecosystem.[142] Apollo has achieved notable milestones, including successfully deploying autonomous taxis in Beijing and other major cities. The project combines AI, big data, and cloud computing to enhance driving algorithms and safety measures.[143]

EHang, another key player in China, focuses on autonomous aerial vehicles (AAVs).[144] The company's

---

[142] https://www.eetimes.com/chinas-apollo-plan-explained/

[143] https://www.theneweconomy.com/strategy/baidu-launches-apollo-self-driving-platform

[144] https://www.wipo.int/wipo_magazine/en/ip-at-work/2021/ehang.html

EHang 216, a two-seater drone, has undergone extensive testing, including passenger trials and logistical operations. EHang's efforts prove a major step toward integrating aerial and ground transportation. [145] [146] As a result, there is immense potential to alleviate urban congestion and offer new modes of travel for the growing population already pressuring the current transportation infrastructure.[147]

Europe's Regulatory and Technological Landscape Subject to Change

In Europe, initiatives like the UK's GATEway Project and Sweden's Drive Me trial demonstrate efforts to advance autonomous driving technology while navigating regulatory challenges.[148] The GATEway Project, based in Greenwich, London, explores the integration of autonomous vehicles into public transportation networks.[149] It aims to demonstrate how these vehicles can operate safely and efficiently in mixed-traffic environments. Similarly, Sweden's Drive Me project focuses on real-world trials of autonomous vehicles on public roads, intending to assess their performance and societal impact.[150]

---

[145]https://www.ehang.com/app/en/EHang%20White%20Paper%20on%20Urban%20Air%20Mobility%20Systems.pdf

[146]https://www.forbes.com/sites/johnkoetsier/2023/10/13/global-first-autonomous-passenger-drone-gets-approval-to-fly/

[147] https://ieeexplore.ieee.org/abstract/document/10343091/

[148]https://www.rca.ac.uk/research-innovation/projects/gateway-driverless-transport/

[149] https://fseg.gre.ac.uk/fire/gateway.html

[150]https://www.researchgate.net/publication/309066480_When_Autonomous_Vehiclesre_Introduced_on_a_Larger_Scale_in_the_Road_Transport_System_The_Drive_Me_Project

However, the widespread adoption of autonomous vehicles in Europe has faced growing challenges. The varying differences in regulatory frameworks across different countries have been a concern for AV technology pioneers. This issue has become an increasingly challenging obstacle for companies seeking to deploy autonomous technology universally. Moreover, public acceptance remains a critical issue, with concerns about the safety and reliability of autonomous systems influencing regulatory decisions and consumer attitudes.[151][152]

Personalization in Mobility for Tailored Commuter Experiences

The need for personalization in mobility has also grown significantly, transforming each journey into a unique experience tailored to the individual preferences and needs of the consumer. Therefore, leading companies' tech advancements focus on enhancing in-car technology and mobile apps. Systems like Mercedes-Benz's MBUX and BMW's color-changing technology are great examples that indicate how personalization enhances both comfort and aesthetic appeal.

---

[151]https://www.researchgate.net/publication/346178076_Individual_Predict ors_of_Autonomous_Vehicle_Public_Acceptance_and_Intention_to_Use_A_S ystematic_Review_of_the_Literature

[152]https://www.researchgate.net/publication/343306283_Using_the_UTAU T2_model_to_explain_public_acceptance_of_conditionally_automated_L3_car s_A_questionnaire_study_among_9118_car_drivers_from_eight_European_co untries

Meanwhile, mobile apps like Google Maps and Waze and international innovations like Toyota's mood-recognizing technology and Audi's smart home integration demonstrate the expanding scope of personalization in the mobility sector.

These developments reshape how users interact with their vehicles and create unique travel experiences.

Case Study of Mercedes-Benz MBUX System

Mercedes-Benz's MBUX (Mercedes-Benz User Experience) system represents a significant leap in in-car personalization technology. It was launched in 2018 and integrated advanced voice recognition, artificial intelligence, and touch controls to create a highly personalized driving experience.[153] The system allows users to interact with their vehicle through natural language and can set navigation preferences, control media, and adjust climate settings based on voice commands.

User experiences with MBUX have highlighted its impact on driving comfort and convenience.[154] The system's ability to learn driver preferences over time enhances the driving experience by adjusting to individual needs. For instance, MBUX can memorize frequent destinations and

---

[153]https://www.theverge.com/2024/1/9/24028012/mercedes-benz-mbux-voice-assistant-ai-llm-mbos-ces

[154] https://www.mercedes-benz-markham.ca/the-new-mercedes-benz-s-class/

suggest routes based on driving habits.[155] This personalization improves comfort and enhances safety by allowing drivers to focus on the road rather than manual controls.

Case Study of BMW's Color-Changing Technology

BMW's color-changing technology, introduced in the BMW iX Flow, showcases innovation in vehicle personalization beyond interior features. The technology allows drivers to change the exterior color of their vehicle at the touch of a button. It shifts between shades of white, gray, and black. This is achieved through a special E Ink film applied to the car's surface.[156]

The ability to alter the vehicle's color is an innovative way of personalization. It allows owners to adapt their vehicle's appearance to their preferences or environmental conditions. For example, a lighter color can reflect sunlight and reduce the vehicle's interior temperature, while a darker shade might be preferred for a sleek, sophisticated look.[157] This technology caters to consumer preferences and provides practical vehicle maintenance and climate control benefits.

---

[155]https://mbworld.org/forums/gle-class-v167/832399-mbux-suggested-routes.html

[156] https://www.bmwgroup.com/en/news/general/2022/ixflow.html

[157]https://www.researchgate.net/publication/359497576_Why_do_people_choose_their_car_colours

Emerging Trends in Mobile Apps and Services

Google Maps and Waze have revolutionized route planning through AI and machine learning.[158] Both platforms use sophisticated algorithms to analyze real-time traffic data, user behavior, and historical trends to offer optimized route recommendations.[159] For example, Google Maps can suggest alternative routes based on current traffic conditions and user preferences, such as avoiding tolls or highways.

Integration with other mobility services further enhances the user experience. Google Maps and Waze can synchronize with public transportation schedules, ride-sharing services, and electric vehicle charging stations.[160] This interconnected approach provides a seamless travel experience by consolidating multiple aspects of mobility into a single platform.

In Japan, Toyota has introduced mood-recognizing technology that personalizes the in-car environment based on the driver's emotional state.[161] The technology uses sensors and AI. It configures the system to adjust lighting, music, and climate controls to improve the driver's mood and overall driving experience.[162] This innovative approach

---

[158]https://blog.google/products/maps/google-maps-101-how-ai-helps-predict-traffic-and-determine-routes/

[159]https://www.researchgate.net/publication/317573498_Crowdsourced_Road_Navigation_Concept_Design_and_Implementation

[160]https://www.cnbc.com/2018/11/13/how-to-use-google-waze-for-directions-and-avoiding-traffic.html

[161] https://global.toyota/en/newsroom/corporate/30063126.html

[162] https://media.toyota.co.uk/toyota-defines-future-mobility-concept-series/

highlights the growing trend toward emotional and psychological personalization in mobility.

The Integration of Ground and Air Transportation

Ground and air transportation have been the subject of major innovations. Their integration has given rise to an emerging landscape of urban mobility. There are innovative concepts by leading companies in this novel landscape, like Volocopter's VoloPort and Joby Aviation's eVTOL aircraft. There is also the flying car concept by Alef Aeronautics and the Voom service proposed by Airbus.

These advancements have been showcasing the potential to create a more interconnected and efficient mobility ecosystem where air and ground transportation will complement each other to enhance the overall passenger transportation. These technologies promise to reshape how we navigate and connect within our cities as they develop and mature. More importantly, they offer new possibilities for personal and shared transportation.

Urban Air Mobility Developments – Case Study of Volocopter's VoloPort Concept

Volocopter, a pioneer in urban air mobility, has been at the forefront of developing air taxi solutions with its VoloPort concept. The VoloPort is an infrastructure design that facilitates seamless transitions between ground and aerial transportation. It is located in urban centers where ports are equipped to handle Volocopter's eVTOL (electric

Vertical Takeoff and Landing) aircraft.[163] They are also designed to operate autonomously with minimal noise and emissions.

Volocopter's air taxi trials in cities such as Singapore and Paris are significant steps toward integrating UAM into everyday transport.[164] These trials have demonstrated the viability of using electric air taxis to alleviate congestion and provide faster travel options in urban centers. The potential impact on urban transit is significant because VoloPorts could reduce commute times and ease ground traffic congestion while offering a new dimension of connectivity within cities.[165]

Case Study of Joby Aviation's eVTOL Aircraft

Joby Aviation's eVTOL aircraft represent another major advancement in advanced air mobility (AAM).[166] The company's eVTOL is designed for rapid, quiet, and efficient vertical takeoff and landing. Moreover, it aims to revolutionize urban mobility. The company has enhanced operational efficiency with various technological advancements like longer battery life and improved aerodynamic performance.[167]

---

[163] https://www.mdpi.com/2673-7590/3/3/57

[164] https://link.springer.com/article/10.1007/s13272-024-00733-x

[165] https://www.sciencedirect.com/science/article/pii/S0967070X24000696

[166] https://www.sciencedirect.com/science/article/pii/S2773153723000762

[167]https://www.researchgate.net/publication/330197540_Effects_of_Range _Requirements_and_Battery_Technology_on_Electric_VTOL_Sizing_and_Op erational_Performance

For now, the operational goals for Joby Aviation include establishing a network of air taxi services in major cities and commercial launches in the coming years.[168] However, challenges such as regulatory approvals, infrastructure development, and public acceptance remain the main obstacles. On the contrary, Joby's efforts to address these challenges include rigorous safety testing and collaboration with regulatory bodies to ensure that the integration of eVTOLs into urban airspace is both safe and effective.

Synergies with Ground-Based Transportation

Alef Aeronautics is among the pioneering companies with its innovative "flying car," combining road and air travel capabilities. The Alef Model A is designed to operate like a conventional car on the road, capable of vertical take-off and landing.[169] This dual functionality allows users to seamlessly transition between driving and flying, a novel solution for personal transportation in expanding urban centers worldwide.

Integrating Alef's flying car with existing transportation systems involves addressing several vital factors. These include the development of suitable infrastructure like

---

[168]https://www.bloomberg.com/news/articles/2024-03-22/air-taxi-startup-joby-sees-start-of-dubai-services-before-the-us

[169]https://economictimes.indiatimes.com/news/international/us/electric-flying-car-alef-model-a-heres-all-you-may-want-to-know/articleshow/101423375.cms?from=mdr

vertiports and coordination with existing traffic management systems.[170]

Moreover, its potential integration with ground-based transportation networks could provide users with a more versatile and efficient mobility solution. This can reduce the need for traditional ground-based commutes and potentially minimize traffic congestion.

On the other side, Airbus's Voom service is another innovative approach to integrating air and ground transportation. Voom is a helicopter ride-sharing service designed to complement existing urban transportation solutions. They offer quick aerial transit between key city locations; Voom aims to provide travelers with a premium, time-saving option.[171]

A comparative analysis with ground transportation solutions highlights Voom's potential advantages in reducing travel times and offering direct routes across cities.[172] While ground transportation remains essential for local travel and connectivity, services like Voom can enhance overall mobility by providing high-speed, flexible travel options that bridge gaps in the existing transportation network.

The combination of ground and air personal transportation will reconfigure cities and metropolitan areas

---

[170] https://www.mdpi.com/2673-7590/3/3/57
[171] https://www.mdpi.com/2071-1050/13/4/2217
[172] https://www.sciencedirect.com/science/article/pii/S0968090X21003788

in a way never dreamed of before, boosting economic growth and equity in mobility.

The Role of 5G and Satellite Communications in Mobility Advancements

The deployment of 5G networks in major U.S. cities like Los Angeles and New York has been discussed.[173] In Los Angeles, 5G technology is being integrated into smart city projects to support autonomous vehicles (AVs) and advanced traffic management systems.[174] The low latency and high bandwidth of 5G enable real-time Vehicle-to-Everything (V2X) communications, which are crucial for AVs' safe and efficient operation.[175] These advancements allow for smoother traffic flow, better coordination of public transport, and more responsive city infrastructure.

New York City is similarly leveraging 5G to drive innovation in urban mobility.[176] The network supports various smart infrastructure initiatives, which include real-time traffic monitoring and predictive analytics for public transit systems.[177] The benefits of 5G's low latency and high bandwidth[178] are evident in enhanced response times for traffic signals, improved safety features for AVs, and the

---

[173] https://fastercapital.com/keyword/smart-traffic-management.html

[174] https://www.mdpi.com/2879938

[175] https://www.sciencedirect.com/science/article/pii/S2590198223002270

[176]https://www2.deloitte.com/content/dam/Deloitte/cn/Documents/technology-media-telecommunications/deloitte-cn-tmt-empowering-smart-cities-with-5g-white-paper-en-200702.pdf

[177] https://www.mdpi.com/2032-6653/15/4/171

[178]https://www.intel.com/content/www/us/en/wireless-network/5g-benefits-features.html

facilitation of more seamless and integrated transportation services.[179]

Globally, 5G is transforming mobility systems. The government has spearheaded efforts in South Korea to integrate 5G into passenger transportation.[180] Seoul has been a testing ground for 5G-enabled autonomous buses and smart transportation infrastructure.[181] The deployment of 5G enhances operational efficiency and provides real-time data on traffic conditions. It has also enabled advanced vehicle-to-infrastructure communication.

Furthermore, Japan and Finland are notable for their contributions to 5G-enabled mobility.[182] In Japan, the focus has been on integrating 5G with smart city solutions to improve public transportation efficiency and safety.[183] Finland has implemented 5G to support autonomous vehicle trials and enhance connectivity across its public transportation network.[184] It helped showcase advanced communication technologies' role in creating more responsive and efficient mobility systems.[185]

---

[179]https://www.researchgate.net/publication/365451675_Autonomous_Vehicles_in_5G_and_Beyond_A_Survey

[180] https://www.koreaherald.com/view.php?ud=20190523000662

[181]https://www.nbr.org/wp-content/uploads/pdfs/publications/sr84_networked_benefits_may2020.pdf

[182] https://www.sciencedirect.com/science/article/pii/S2666691X24000277

[183] https://www.lowyinstitute.org/the-interpreter/japan-s-5g-ambitions-quad

[184] https://cris.vtt.fi/ws/portalfiles/portal/71877843/1570847436_final.pdf

[185]https://www.researchgate.net/publication/343577759_The_Role_of_5G_Technologies_Challenges_in_Smart_Cities_and_Intelligent_Transportation_Systems

Satellite Communications for Global Connectivity

Now, we have SpaceX's Starlink project transforming global connectivity with its constellation of Low Earth Orbit (LEO) satellites.[186] Starlink's network provides high-speed internet access to remote and underserved areas, particularly impacting rural mobility.[187] The advancements will bridge the connectivity gap as Starlink plans to provide better navigation, real-time tracking, and communication for vehicles operating in regions that lack traditional infrastructure.

In global logistics, Starlink enhances the efficiency and reliability of freight transportation by providing consistent connectivity for ships, airplanes, and trucks. This connectivity is crucial for real-time tracking, efficient route planning, and improved operational coordination across international supply chains.[188]

The Future of Satellite Communications in Mobility

Satellite communications will also support emerging transportation modes such as air mobility (UAM) and autonomous flying vehicles. Satellite technology can offer wide-area coverage and seamless communication for these new modes of transportation.[189] It can complement the capabilities of our current transportation networks.

---

[186] https://www.space.com/spacex-starlink-satellites.html
[187] https://www.researchgate.net/publication/377231331_The_SpaceX_Starl ink_Satellite_Project_Business_Strategies_and_Perspectives
[188] https://www.ils.be/starlink-technology-helps-container-vessels/
[189] https://www.sciencedirect.com/science/article/pii/S2667325823002418

On the other hand, we have the integration of satellite communications with 5G networks that promises to enhance global mobility by providing a unified communication framework.[190] This synergy will support more reliable and efficient transportation systems while facilitating advanced vehicle-to-everything (V2X) interactions.[191] Furthermore, it can improve overall connectivity across metropolitan, rural, and remote areas.

The more recent advancements in 5G and satellite communications can improve the efforts toward a more interconnected and sustainability-driven transportation landscape. It can influence the future of personalized mobility solutions that reduce commute times and enhance travel experiences.

Overviewing the Brain Behind Mobility – AI

May Mobility employs advanced artificial intelligence (AI) technology to power its autonomous vehicles, which ensures they operate safely and efficiently in complex urban environments. This technology's core is sophisticated perception algorithms that process data from LiDAR, cameras, and radar.

These algorithms enable the detection and classification of various objects, such as pedestrians, vehicles, and

---

[190]https://www.researchgate.net/publication/327923609_Framework_for_U nifying_5G_and_Next_Generation_Satellite_Communications

[191]https://www.researchgate.net/publication/361083804_6G_for_Vehicle-to-Everything_V2X_Communications_Enabling_Technologies_Challenges_and_Oppo rtunities

obstacles, to provide the vehicle with a comprehensive understanding of its surroundings.

Furthermore, a key component of May Mobility's AI system is its proprietary multi-policy decision-making approach. This innovative method allows the AI to evaluate multiple possible actions simultaneously. Then, it selects the best course of action based on criteria such as safety, efficiency, and current driving conditions. This ensures that autonomous vehicles can make informed decisions even in dynamic and unpredictable urban settings.

Path planning algorithms are another critical aspect of May Mobility's AI technology. These algorithms determine the safest and most efficient route for the vehicle. Consequently, these algorithms utilize real-time data and high-definition maps. Continuously analyzing the environment allows the AI to adjust the vehicle's path to avoid obstacles and respond to changing traffic conditions.

The AI-driven control systems are responsible for executing driving decisions in real-time. These systems manage the vehicles' acceleration, braking, and steering to ensure smooth and safe navigation. Additionally, May Mobility uses machine learning to improve its AI system continuously. The vehicles learn from each trip. This enhances their performance and helps the AI-powered models adapt to new scenarios. Waymo has been leveraging advanced AI algorithms to improve the decision-making capabilities of its AV technology. The deployed AVs, therefore, could significantly improve road safety and commute experiences for travelers by making real-time decisions with accurate information.

Waymo's AI system uses a combination of machine learning, computer vision, and sensor technology to interpret complex driving environments. These algorithms enable the vehicle to make real-time decisions based on camera, lidar, and radar data.[192] As a result, it significantly improves safety by predicting and responding to dynamic road conditions.

Mercedes-Benz is integrating AI into its European vehicles to enhance driver assistance systems.[193] Mercedes-Benz's AI-powered systems offer adaptive cruise control and lane-keeping assistance to improve vehicle safety and driving comfort.[194] In China, NIO is utilizing AI to enhance its autonomous driving capabilities. NIO's AI-driven system, NIO Pilot, uses deep learning algorithms to improve navigation and decision-making in various driving scenarios.[195]

The future of AI in autonomous mobility is promising due to ongoing research focused on refining AI algorithms for better adaptability and safety. AI-driven predictive maintenance and improved sensor technology integration

---

[192]https://www.sciencedirect.com/science/article/abs/pii/S000145752200358X

[193] https://www.benzinsider.com/2023/08/how-mercedes-benz-ai-is-revolutionizing-luxury-vehicles/

[194] https://www.theverge.com/2023/9/27/23892154/mercedes-benz-drive-pilot-autonomous-level-3-test

[195] https://www.mdpi.com/2032-6653/14/9/251

can further enhance the capabilities of autonomous vehicles.[196]

Traffic Flow Optimization and Smart Management

AI has been engaging more than individual vehicles. It has widespread applications, primarily urban traffic management, as we have learned through various case studies and real-world examples in the previous chapters. [197] [198]

Singapore was a leading example of how AI can optimize traffic flow and reduce congestion.[199] The city-state employs an AI-driven traffic management system that uses real-time data to adjust traffic signals and manage traffic flow.[200] This system has successfully reduced congestion and improved public transportation efficiency by ensuring smoother traffic conditions and timely updates to transit schedules.

The benefits of AI in traffic management are mainly seen through reduced travel times and enhanced public transit reliability. The AI systems analyze traffic patterns and predict congestion to proactively manage traffic and lead to

---

[196] https://www.sciencedirect.com/science/article/pii/S0045790624001654

[197] https://biotechjournal.org/index.php/jbai/article/view/67

[198] https://www.researchgate.net/profile/Chirag-Shah-44/publication/381417014_Physics_Model-Based_Design_for_Predictive_Maintenance_in_Autonomous_Vehicles_Using_AI/links/666c59d6a54c5f0b946514b1/Physics-Model-Based-Design-for-Predictive-Maintenance-in-Autonomous-Vehicles-Using-AI.pdf

[199] https://eudl.eu/pdf/10.4108/ew.4613

[200] https://www.jetir.org/papers/JETIR2407235.pdf

more efficient and responsive metropolitan transportation networks.

Moreover, applications like Google Maps and Waze use AI algorithms to provide personalized route recommendations based on real-time traffic data and user preferences. These apps continuously learn from user interactions and traffic conditions to optimize routing and enhance the travel experience.[201]

AI has the potential to create even more seamless travel experiences. Future developments may include AI-driven multi-modal transportation solutions that integrate various transportation modes into a user-friendly platform, further personalizing and streamlining the travel experience.[202]

Autonomous vehicles and advanced in-car technologies integrating ground and air transportation systems can significantly boost metropolitan mobility developments. They are vital to addressing modern transportation challenges and shifting consumer demands.

Moreover, the growing correlation between 5G facilities and satellite communications can impact mobility solutions in the world's dense urban centers. Although continuous development will be highly valued in the coming years to use these evolving concepts, they can streamline transit and

---

[201] https://www.researchgate.net/publication/334461804_Human-computer_trust_in_navigation_systems_google_maps_vs_waze
[202] https://ijsrm.net/index.php/ijsrm/article/download/5072/3152/14950

help us achieve a more connected and responsive metropolitan environment.

Transportation providers, both private and governmental, will gain access to a groundbreaking technology catalyst that will revolutionize their operations. This technology will empower them to make significant advancements, enhancing all models and fostering larger cooperative ecosystems. As a result, they will be able to outpace competitors and achieve rapid and substantial growth in their operations as the future of mobility becomes increasingly Electric, Autonomous, Connected, and Personalized.

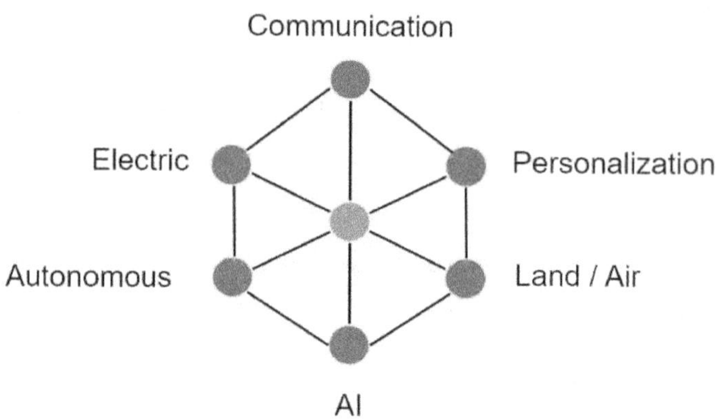

Cost Reductions and Personal Mobility

The convergence of technology will reduce operational costs and shift from massive to personal mobility.

Regarding operational costs, the rise of autonomous vehicles (AVs) and safer driving technologies is driving significant changes in the insurance industry, reshaping risk assessments, coverage options, and liability structures.

With fewer accidents expected due to advanced driver assistance systems (ADAS) and autonomous technologies, insurance premiums are anticipated to decrease. These technologies shift responsibility away from human error, making it necessary for insurers to focus more on product liability—where car manufacturers and software providers may bear responsibility for accidents instead of drivers. As a result, companies like Tesla have begun partnering with insurers such as Liberty Mutual to offer custom policies tailored to autonomous features, lowering risks and adjusting premiums accordingly.

The industry is evolving towards models that rely heavily on real-time driving data from telematics systems. This data allows insurers to personalize premiums based on driving habits, such as acceleration and braking behavior, ensuring more precise underwriting. Furthermore, as more autonomous vehicles enter the market, some insurance liability is expected to shift to commercial policies, particularly for commercial fleets and self-driving trucks, which will soon dominate highways.

Insurers are adapting by hiring data scientists and AI specialists to refine risk models for the new technologies. Companies like Allstate are actively investing in research on AV safety to remain competitive in this rapidly evolving space. However, the transition is not without challenges, including regulatory uncertainties and the potential reduction in traditional auto insurance revenue as accident rates decline and liability shifts.

The convergence of technology, safety improvements, and regulatory adjustments is transforming the insurance landscape and presenting opportunities for insurers who can innovate and adapt to this new mobility era.

Consulting firms such as McKinsey, Deloitte, and Boston Consulting Group (BCG) predict that electric vehicles (EVs) and autonomous vehicles (AVs) will significantly reduce costs over the coming decade, transforming mobility and disrupting traditional transportation systems.

McKinsey forecasts that by 2030, improvements in battery technology and manufacturing processes will reduce the total cost of ownership for EVs to match or even undercut that of internal combustion engine vehicles.[203] This decline will be driven by economies of scale, improved energy efficiency, and government incentives for sustainable transport. The report also predicts that shared AVs could reduce per-mile transportation costs by up to 40% in urban areas, especially when integrated into mass transit networks to optimize utilization and minimize downtime.[204]

Deloitte highlights that integrating autonomous technologies with public transportation—such as on-demand shuttles or vehicles—will enhance operational efficiency

---

[203]https://www.mckinsey.com/industries/financial-services/our-insights/connected-revolution-the-future-of-us-auto-insurance

[204]https://www.mckinsey.com/industries/automotive-and-assembly/our-insights/autonomous-drivings-future-convenient-and-connected

and cut labor costs. These savings could allow transit agencies to expand service coverage without increasing fares, promoting accessibility and sustainability.[205]

Projects like Arlington, Texas's RAPID service demonstrate how AVs can complement traditional mass transit by addressing "last-mile" connectivity. These systems enable transit agencies to serve a broader population with fewer resources, reducing congestion and emissions.[206]

BCG projects that by 2030, EVs could account for up to 30% of new vehicle sales in the U.S. under optimal conditions.[207] AVs will be increasingly important in both public and private transportation sectors. However, automakers and transit operators will need further policy support, charging infrastructure investments, and continue technological advancements to achieve these cost reductions and market penetration. These insights suggest that future mobility solutions leveraging AV and EV technologies will reduce costs and improve sustainability and accessibility, shifting to personal over mass mobility.

As we close this chapter, we see how technology and innovation have become the keystones propelling mobility into the future. The convergence of electrification, AI, personalization, communications, and autonomous systems

---

[205]https://outsideinsight.com/insights/how-autonomous-vehicles-are-impacting-the-insurance-industry/

[206]https://www.bcg.com/publications/2017/reimagined-car-shared-autonomous-electric

[207]https://www.bcg.com/publications/2017/automotive-making-autonomous-vehicles-a-reality

heralds an era of exponential growth, where transportation seamlessly integrates ground and air travel and anticipates users' needs in real time.

However, as we forge ahead with such groundbreaking technological strides, a pivotal question remains: How do we balance the rapid pace of innovation with equitable access to resources? This brings us to the next chapter, Abundance vs. Scarcity mindset, where we will explore the challenges and opportunities inherent in ensuring that technological advancements serve not just a few but benefit society as a whole.

Chapter 11
Mindset Shift:
Unlocking Mobility's Potential by Embracing Abundance Over Scarcity

"The key to abundance is meeting limited circumstances with unlimited thoughts."

-Marianne Williamson

The concepts of abundance and scarcity offer contrasting perspectives. They are both vital for shaping strategies, innovations, and market approaches. However, in the expanding mobility industry, they can influence how passenger transportation providers approach solution value, resource allocation, and consumer needs-driven solutions in the new Post-Digital economy.

Scarcity refers to a model where resources are limited. This leads to heightened competition and often results in higher costs and restricted access. This Classic Economy model, discussed in Chapter 3, was more prevalent in the passenger transportation sector, where physical constraints and regulatory frameworks have now acted as barriers to entry and growth.

For example, the traditional taxi sector was limited due to a set number of medallions or licenses. This defined the scarcity in the growing market with shifting consumer behaviors. It indicated how controlling the supply of available taxis could help companies inflate prices and limit service accessibility.

On the other hand, abundance signifies a shift toward leveraging technology and innovative business models to overcome traditional constraints. It emphasizes maximizing resource utilization and expanding access to services or product solutions. It also fosters collaborative solutions that enhance efficiency and reduce costs, aligning with the Post-Digital Economy model discussed in Chapter 3.

A good example is the rise of digital platforms like ride-sharing services and mobility-as-a-service (MaaS) solutions. It shows an abundance model where platforms leverage technology to pool resources, optimize routing, and create more dynamic and accessible transportation options for commuters. GNET is leveraging an international vehicle ecosystem to create an always-available experience for private transportation providers' passengers in the Livery business.

This chapter will focus on that. We will understand how transitioning from a scarcity to an abundance model in the mobility industry can lead to significant developments. Additionally, we will discuss which ongoing advancements and changes are impacting this potential transition to address contemporary mobility challenges.

The Scarcity Model and Its Historical Constraints and Impact on Mobility

We look at New York City's taxi medallion system, established in the early 20th century. It is a typical example of the scarcity model in the transportation sector. Under this system, the city issues a finite number of medallions, similar to licenses necessary for operating taxis. Based on this regulatory framework, the authorities could control the number of taxis circulating on the road. Though allegedly, it seemingly was to ensure quality and manage congestion.

However, the medallion system created artificial scarcity. This happened when the demand for taxi services grew, and the limited supply of medallions drove up their value significantly. By 2014, the price of a medallion had soared to over $1 million.[208] This high cost of entry prevented new taxi operators from entering the market, and the resulting scarcity led to higher fares for consumers.

The scarcity of medallions led to lower market competition, which made service availability and pricing issues an even bigger challenge for the standard user. The high cost of obtaining a medallion went on toward the passenger in the form of higher fares as taxi operators tried to recover or break even from the high initial investment.

---

[208] https://hrlr.law.columbia.edu/hrlr-online/distressed-drivers-solving-the-new-york-city-taxi-medallion-debtcrisis/#:~:text=In%202014%2C%20just%20as%20Uber,medallion%20dropped%20to%20approximately%20%24600%2C000.

This made taxi services more autonomous and less accessible, particularly for lower-income individuals.[209]

In recent years, the medallion system has faced increasing criticism.[210] Introducing ride-sharing services was highly important in exposing the inefficiencies and shortcomings of the medallion model.[211] As a result, there has been a significant shift in the regulatory landscape with ongoing debates about balancing innovation, competition, and consumer protection.

Analyzing the Impact of Black Cars and Limousines in Urban Circulation

The black car and limousine sector, rising due to luxury and exclusivity, has also operated under a scarcity model.[212] The licensing constraints and operational permissions were the main limiting factors to the industry's growth and flexibility in this sector.

In many cities, black car and limousine services are subject to stringent regulations restricting the number of operators and vehicles allowed to operate. These regulations were initially implemented to ensure high standards and prevent market saturation.[213]

---

[209] https://www.reuters.com/article/world/why-taxi-medallions-cost-1-million-idUS1274642834/

[210] https://www.rstreet.org/commentary/nycs-taxi-medallion-crisis-is-a-case-study-in-government-malfeasance/

[211] https://dl.acm.org/doi/fullHtml/10.1145/3178876.3186134

[212] https://www.nyc.gov/assets/tlc/downloads/pdf/annual_report_2021.pdf

[213] https://onlinepubs.trb.org/onlinepubs/sr/sr319AppendixB.pdf

For instance, there are complex bureaucratic processes and significant costs for licensing black cars and limousines in cities like San Francisco and Los Angeles.[214] These constraints serve as limiting factors and prevent a sustainable increase in the available services. Moreover, they also increase operational costs, which often translates into higher service costs for consumers.

The need to comply with regulatory standards and maintain a fleet of luxury vehicles led to elevated service prices. As a result, the consumer base for black car and limousine services was restricted to those who could afford the premium pricing. Hence, it led to reduced accessibility for the general public.

Moreover, these constraints have often led to a lack of flexibility in service offerings. The need to adhere to strict regulations and high operational costs made it difficult for providers to innovate or adapt to changing market demands, further entrenching the scarcity model.

Scarcity in Private Transit Fleets

Private transit fleets like those operated by corporations and educational institutions also faced constraints related to the scarcity model. Vehicle availability, driver recruitment, and funding often constrain these fleets. Companies and institutions operating private transit services must manage a finite number of vehicles and drivers. This again limits the

---

[214] http://research.gsd.harvard.edu/tut/files/2016/06/San-Francisco-Case-2016.pdf

ability to scale services to ensure a shrink or expansion based on consumer demands.

For example, corporate fleets are typically designed to transport employees between office locations, campuses, or transit hubs. Budgetary limits and logistical challenges often constrain the availability of such vehicles and their drivers.[215] Many companies struggle to balance the cost of maintaining a fleet with the need for reliable transportation services. And that leads to significant management challenges in areas that experience fluctuating demands.[216]

Similarly, educational institutions with private transit fleets face challenges in managing vehicle availability and driver recruitment. Schools and universities often operate fleets to transport students and staff. Still, there are financial constraints and regulatory requirements with the management of these fleets, which automatically limits their ability to expand services.[217] Funding limitations may restrict the number of vehicles that can be acquired or maintained. Meanwhile, there are difficulties in recruiting qualified drivers, which negatively impacts the reliability and flexibility of the service.

The constraints imposed by the scarcity model in private transit fleets have often led to challenges in scaling services to meet growing demand. As a result, these fleets may

---

[215] https://rosap.ntl.bts.gov/view/dot/3811/dot_3811_DS1.pdf?
[216] https://www3.weforum.org/docs/WEF_Corporate_Mobility_Transport_Challenge_Report.pdf
[217] https://direct.mit.edu/edfp/article/18/2/351/110633/Student-Transportation-in-Choice-Rich-Districts

struggle to provide adequate coverage or adapt to changes in transportation needs. This further highlights the limitations of the scarcity model in the mobility landscape.

However, the advent of digital technology and the sharing economy challenges the traditional scarcity model in the passenger transportation sector. Ride-sharing platforms and other mobility-as-a-service (MaaS) solutions are beginning to overcome the physical and regulatory constraints that have historically limited the industry. By leveraging technology to pool resources, optimize routing, and match supply with demand more efficiently, these new models promise to unlock more transportation options, reducing costs, increasing accessibility, and fostering innovation in a sector long governed by scarcity principles.

The Transition from Scarcity to Abundance Models

Ride-sharing platforms have been key players in addressing the shift from the scarcity model to the abundance model in the mobility industry. These platforms use advanced technology to optimize vehicle utilization and address traffic congestion. Therefore, it helps effectively transform how transportation services are delivered.

These platforms use sophisticated algorithms and real-time data analytics to match drivers with passengers. As a result, it maximizes vehicle utilization. The platform aggregates rides from multiple users to increase the efficiency of each vehicle on the road.

This also leads to reduced number of empty or underutilized vehicles. Furthermore, this optimization helps minimize traffic congestion and reduce operational costs. This can be passed on to consumers through lower fares or subscription fees.[218]

The impact of ride-sharing on transportation choices is profound.[219] For instance, Uber's data indicates that their service has led to a 10% reduction in personal vehicle ownership in major cities like San Francisco.[220] This shift reduces traffic congestion and pollution as fewer private vehicles are needed.[221] Additionally, ride-sharing platforms

---

[218]https://www.researchgate.net/publication/322605779_Ridesourcing_the_sharing_economy_and_the_future_of_cities
[219] https://www.nrel.gov/docs/fy21osti/78293.pdf
[220] https://www.sciencedirect.com/science/article/pii/S2589004220311305
[221] https://www.ncbi.nlm.nih.gov/pmc/articles/PMC7835256/

have introduced features like carpooling and electric vehicle options, which bring environmental benefits into the mix.

Furthermore, transportation accessibility has improved because ride-sharing services offer affordable alternatives to traditional taxis and public transit.[222] This increased accessibility is particularly beneficial in underserved areas where traditional transportation options may be limited. With the availability of such transportation choices at varying and affordable price points, these ride-sharing platforms support a more inclusive mobility ecosystem.

Real-World Examples – MAGIIS Autonomous Open Ecosystem

MAGIIS Autonomous Open Marketplace represents a groundbreaking approach to addressing current and future global mobility challenges. This innovative system is an end-to-end digital software platform designed to enhance customer engagement through an omnichannel interface, streamline providers' back-office operations with world-class processes, and transform providers' collaboration with its Vehicles Open Marketplace.

The white-label platform enables mobility service providers to connect across different regions, facilitating vehicle sharing and service coordination on an autonomous global scale. Providers can share online vehicles across borders, ensuring passengers an "Always Available

---

[222] https://www.sciencedirect.com/science/article/pii/S0965856421002809

Experience" and significantly increasing transportation service efficiency through autonomous dispatching.

The autonomous technology embedded in MAGIIS's Marketplace represents a quantum leap forward in global mobility. It redefines how vehicles are shared globally by connecting to any available ecosystem worldwide. The platform can dispatch multiple vehicles and services, supporting the emerging autonomous vehicle technologies set to transform how consumers move globally.

MAGIIS incorporates a native Mobility as a Service (MaaS) technology that fosters extreme collaboration, driving innovation and enhancing the overall mobility industry. By doing so, MAGIIS acts as a catalyst for advancing the abundance model within the Passenger Transportation sector, ensuring sustainable growth and efficiency.

MAGIIS is not just a technological advancement but a strategic enabler of global mobility, setting new benchmarks and driving the future of transportation forward.

Growing Innovations in Autonomous Vehicles

Waymo's self-driving cars also employ a combination of advanced sensors, machine learning algorithms, and real-time data processing to move through complex driving environments autonomously.[223] This technology can

---

[223] https://www.sciencedirect.com/science/article/pii/S2590005621000059

potentially revolutionize the mobility industry by reducing the cost of vehicle ownership and increasing accessibility.

The advancements in Waymo's technology have led to significant improvements in the cost and availability of transportation services. It eliminates the need for a human driver as Waymo's vehicles can operate more continuously. This optimizes vehicle utilization and reduces the overall service costs to minimize commuters' costs. This efficiency can make transportation more affordable and accessible to a broader population.

May Mobility formed strategic partnerships with cities and businesses to integrate its shuttles into existing transportation networks. This collaborative approach helped it streamline deployment and adoption. Meanwhile, it enhanced the overall effectiveness of their solutions.

It also emphasized user-friendly design and convenience to ensure its vehicles met the needs of passengers. For the company, the ultimate goal was passenger safety and commute reliability.

Emergence of Autonomous Taxis in Shenzhen

AutoX, a Chinese autonomous vehicle startup, has made significant strides in deploying fully autonomous taxis in Shenzhen.[224] These autonomous taxis utilize cutting-edge technology to operate safely and efficiently in one of the

---

[224] https://www.szpsq.gov.cn/english/PingshanHigh-techZoneaimsforglobalstatus/content/post_8686521.html

world's most densely urban environments.[225] AutoX's implementation of autonomous taxis represents a crucial step forward in demonstrating the viability of self-driving technology in real-world conditions.

Innovations in digital technology and autonomous vehicle industries mainly fuel the transition from a scarcity model to an abundance model in mobility. There is a need for innovative and transformative ideas that utilize evolving technology. As a result, the mobility service providers in the industry will have better knowledge and tools to optimize vehicle utilization, enhance service efficiency, and expand accessibility.

Active and Practical Abundance Models in the Mobility Industry

Mobile applications like Google Maps and Citymapper integrate various transportation modes into a single platform, fostering the abundance model. These apps leverage data from public transit, ride-sharing services, bike-sharing programs, and walking routes to provide users with travel solutions.[226]

These applications can consolidate multiple transportation options into one interface. In turn, it optimizes travel planning and enhances user convenience. Google Maps, for instance, offers real-time information on public transit

---

[225] https://www.forbes.com/sites/suzannerowankelleher/2020/12/03/video-watch-chinas-first-fleet-of-driverless-robotaxis-hits-shenzhen/
[226] https://www.sciencedirect.com/science/article/pii/S2590198222001324

schedules, ride-sharing availability, and bike-sharing locations.[227] This allows users to choose the most efficient route based on current conditions.[228]

This integration helps users reduce travel time and increases their accessibility to transportation services. Similarly, Citymapper provides detailed route planning that combines various modes of transportation like subways, buses, ferries, and ridesharing options to offer users the fastest and most convenient travel routes. [229] [230]

These multi-modal platforms improve and enhance user convenience through one-stop mobility solutions for easier travel planning and access to sustainable transportation solutions for travel planning. They also promote sustainable transportation modes by highlighting biking or public transit options.

The Role of EVs, AVs, and Sustainability-Driven Transportation Practices

Electric vehicles (EVs) and sustainable practices are central to the abundance model in transportation driven by EV technology and infrastructure innovations.[231] Companies like Tesla and Rivian are developing EVs with advanced

---

[227] https://www.theverge.com/2019/8/27/20835131/google-maps-combine-transit-biking-ride-sharing

[228] https://www.latimes.com/travel/story/2019-07-17/google-maps-real-time-bike-share-availability

[229] https://fastercapital.com/topics/mobility-as-a-service-(maas):-integrating-various-modes-of-transportation.html

[230]https://unece.org/DAM/trans/doc/2019/itc/Informal_document_No_2_MaaS.pdf

[231] https://www.sciencedirect.com/science/article/pii/S0967070X20309495

battery technology and expanding charging infrastructure to support widespread adoption.[232]

Tesla's advancements in battery technology, like its Gigafactory and innovations in battery chemistry, have been significantly improving the performance of electric vehicles.[233] The expansion of fast-charging networks and the introduction of ultra-fast charging stations further support the viability of EVs for long-distance travel to address one of the major barriers to adoption.[234]

Furthermore, Tesla's planned Robotaxi launch represents a tectonic shift in the mobility industry, propelling it from an era of scarcity into one of abundance. The abundance model is a central theme of Mobility 3.0, highlighting how technological disruption, particularly in autonomous transportation, can elevate global mobility to unprecedented availability, efficiency, and sustainability levels.

Historically, passenger transportation has been bound by limitations: cost, human labor, availability of vehicles, and operational inefficiencies. Tesla's robotaxi—designed to be fully autonomous with no steering wheel or pedals and aimed at a cost-effective price point under $30,000—signals a significant disruption of these constraints[235]. This transition from human-driven vehicles to autonomous fleets

---

[232] https://www.iea.org/reports/global-ev-outlook-2024/trends-in-electric-cars
[233] https://www.reuters.com/technology/gigacasting-20-tesla-reinvents-carmaking-with-quiet-breakthrough-2023-09-14/
[234] https://www.sciencedirect.com/science/article/abs/pii/S0301421521002421
[235] https://technologymagazine.com/articles/teslas-cybercab-robotaxi-using-ai-for-autonomous-vehicles

promises to lower costs for end-users, offering greater accessibility and democratizing mobility options. The cost-per-mile for robotaxis is expected to plummet, enabling people from diverse economic backgrounds to access on-demand transportation.

Autonomous vehicles like Robotaxi can operate 24/7 without fatigue, enabling higher utilization rates than human-driven cars. Unlike conventional taxi or ride-share models, which are often limited by driver availability, Robotaxi fleets can be operational around the clock. This seamless availability reduces waiting times and increases service reliability, which is key to creating a truly abundant mobility network. No longer will passengers be constrained by limited peak-hour availability; instead, they will experience a robust, "Always Available" transportation service.

The shift towards autonomous electric vehicles goes beyond just convenience it redefines our approach to sustainability. By prioritizing electric, emission-free propulsion, Tesla's Robotaxi fleet offers a cleaner alternative to traditional combustion vehicles. This change directly addresses climate challenges, reducing our collective carbon footprint and accelerating the adoption of sustainable mobility solutions.

Moreover, Tesla's ambitions will spur economic abundance within the industry. Infrastructure investments, such as charging stations and maintenance hubs, will be necessary to support large Robotaxi fleets, creating new jobs and economic activity. For those companies willing to innovate, the transition will open doors to new revenue streams and collaborative opportunities that were previously unimaginable.

The abundance model described in Mobility 3.0 thrives on collaboration. Tesla's efforts will inevitably create an ecosystem where software developers, energy companies, regulatory bodies, and mobility providers collaborate to co-create solutions. Tesla's robotaxi fleets will support and interact with diverse platforms and infrastructures, driving market interdependence and fostering extreme collaboration. This concept is foundational to the success of the Mobility as a Service (MaaS) paradigm: cooperation rather than isolation, shared resources over proprietary silos.

While the vision is compelling, challenges remain. Regulatory complexities and safety standards are a continual hurdle[236], but they underscore the importance of resilient and adaptive industry leaders. Competition from Waymo and May Mobility will demand Tesla's innovation to differentiate itself through customer experience and technological supremacy.

Tesla's robotaxi embodies the ideals of Mobility 3.0 by redefining how we move, who has access to it, and the collaborative structures required to sustain it. It is not just about introducing a new service but about enabling abundance for millions of passengers and creating a mobility

---

[236]https://techcrunch.com/2024/10/17/beyond-the-hype-why-teslas-robotaxi-future-faces-regulatory-roadblocks/

ecosystem that supports a brighter, greener, and more interconnected future.

Future Trends and Emerging Technologies

Air Mobility (UAM) initiatives like those by Volocopter and Joby Aviation, which we discussed earlier, showcase a significant move toward integrating air and ground transportation models. Introducing advanced, multi-modal mobility solutions is also a major leap toward an abundance model. Volocopter's air taxi concept can provide on-demand aerial transportation within metropolitan areas while utilizing electric vertical take-off and landing (eVTOL) technology to navigate cityscapes.[237]

Volocopter's VoloCity is designed to address metropolitan congestion by providing a new layer of mobility that operates above-ground traffic.[238] The potential impact on metropolitan transit is significant because UAM can reduce travel times and decrease the pressure on ground-based transportation systems. Similarly, Joby Aviation's eVTOL aircraft offers a promising solution for air travel, focusing on efficiency, low noise, and environmental sustainability.[239]

---

[237]https://www.researchgate.net/publication/346104023_Air_taxi_service_f or_urban_mobility_A_critical_review_of_recent_developments_future_challen ges_and_opportunities

[238]https://www.researchgate.net/publication/365342545_Urban_air_mobilit y_and_flying_cars_Overview_examples_prospects_drawbacks_and_solutions

[239] https://www.sciencedirect.com/science/article/pii/S2773153723000762

However, the integration of UAM with existing ground transportation poses several challenges. These include issues related to air traffic management, safety regulations, and public acceptance, which need to be addressed to realize the full potential of air mobility.[240]

We understand that shifting from a scarcity model to an abundance model in the mobility industry will lead to a significant transformation.

---

[240] https://www.sciencedirect.com/science/article/pii/S1366554522002496

It will impact the service development and delivery for commuters in smart cities, metropolitan and rural areas. However, advancing digital technology and innovative business practices implemented by providers will be key in maximizing the opportunities in the coming years.

As we have explored in this chapter, the future of mobility is laden with both immense opportunities and intricate challenges. The ride-hailing sector has already witnessed disruptive innovation, and as it rapidly evolves, newcomers have a unique window to compete against established industry giants by embracing an abundant mindset. This mindset, focused on collaboration, openness, and leveraging technology at scale, has the potential to reshape competitive landscapes, turning what was once scarcity into boundless possibilities. However, this transformation represents only the initial stages of a broader revolution driven by technological advancements.

The journey does not stop with ride-hailing alone. Next on the horizon lies the livery, bus, coach, and microtransit sectors—all primed for disruption and reinvention through emerging mobility technologies. While technology serves as a crucial enabler for change, it is insufficient to thrive in the "post-digital economy." Adopting the latest advancements without addressing foundational organizational elements will not lead to long-term success. True abundance in people transportation demands more than automated fleets, AI-powered logistics, and digital apps. It requires a holistic transformation across organizational structures, culture, processes, and collaboration networks.

The following chapter will delve deeper into the additional dimensions required to foster exponential growth within the passenger transportation sector.

Chapter 12
Organizational Abundance: Meeting the Demands of a Rapidly Growing People Transportation Sector

"If you want to go fast, go alone. If you want to go far, go together."

-African Proverb

Organizations must radically reimagine their operational frameworks to fully unlock the transformative power of the abundance model in the mobility industry.

This journey requires a shift in mindset and a deep commitment to embracing an abundant model at every level—fostering abundant-minded tribes, setting ambitious yet attainable KPIs, and integrating cutting-edge, abundance-driven technologies.

Through compelling real-world examples from the United States and beyond, this narrative explores how pioneering organizations are leading the charge toward a more inclusive, sustainable, and innovative future in people's transportation.

However, the traditional scarcity model focuses on managing limited resources, while the abundance model seeks to maximize potential by creating an environment where resources are utilized creatively and sustainably. This shift is vital in the current era, where environmental concerns, technological advancements, and changing consumer expectations seriously impact the mobility industry. Organizational change has become crucial for the successful adoption of the abundance model. Companies must realign their operational strategies, culture, and goals to adopt this new way of thinking. This would involve rethinking traditional business practices and integrating principles for long-term value over short-term gains.

Moreover, adopting the abundance model will require organizations to commit to sustainability. They will also have to demonstrate efforts toward innovation and scalability, with consumer-centric approaches being the core components of their operational frameworks.

It is essential to understand that sustainability is not an ethical obligation but a strategic advantage for enhancing a company's market position in the current business environment. On the other hand, innovation seems crucial for staying ahead in a competitive industry.

That is because technological advancements and evolving consumer needs have become an influential factor. Furthermore, scalability is helping to ensure that solutions are effective on a small scale and capable of being expanded to meet growing demand.

With a consumer-centric approach that focuses on understanding and addressing the needs and preferences of users, companies can achieve higher customer satisfaction and loyalty. Moreover, these elements are the foundation of the abundance model in the passenger transportation sector.

The Adoption of the Abundance Model in the Mobility Industry

Today, sustainability is no longer a secondary consideration. It is a central component of modern business strategies, especially in the passenger transportation sector. The main factors behind this shift are regulatory requirements, changing consumer preferences, and the need for long-term economic viability.

However, the adoption of sustainable practices in transportation will have several key aspects. These will include reducing carbon emissions, enhancing energy efficiency, and leveraging renewable energy sources. For now, the companies that prioritize these principles are contributing to environmental preservation and also working to achieve economic benefits through cost savings and improved operational efficiencies.

The Impact of Tesla on Electric Vehicles

Tesla, Inc., a leader in the electric vehicle (EV) market, is a prime example of how sustainability can be embedded into a business model. It was founded to accelerate the world's transition to sustainable energy. And ever since, Tesla has pioneered advancements in electric mobility, battery technology, and renewable energy integration.

Tesla's sustainable practices are multifaceted. The company's core product line comprises electric vehicles producing zero tailpipe emissions. This is a significant step toward reducing the environmental impact of personal transportation. According to Tesla's 2023 Impact Report, EVs have collectively avoided over 2.7 million metric tons of CO2 emissions annually.[241] This figure is equivalent to removing about 550,000 gasoline-powered vehicles from the road, highlighting the substantial environmental benefits of Tesla's vehicles.

Tesla's innovation in battery technology has also played a crucial role in enhancing the economic viability of electric vehicles. According to a report, the cost of lithium-ion batteries has dropped by 89% over the past decade.[242]

This significant reduction in battery costs has made EVs more affordable for consumers and has accelerated their adoption across various markets.[243] The report highlights

---

[241] https://www.tesla.com/ns_videos/2021-tesla-impact-report.pdf

[242] https://www.fullstackeconomics.com/p/untitled-2

[243] https://about.bnef.com/blog/lithium-ion-battery-pack-prices-hit-record-low-of-139-kwh/

that Tesla's continuous improvements in battery efficiency and cost have been instrumental in driving down the overall price of EVs. This has made them more competitive with traditional internal combustion engine vehicles bringing abundance to the EV vehicle industry.

The Role of BYD in Mobility

BYD Auto Co. Ltd., also a prominent player in the electric vehicle industry, has taken significant steps toward transforming metropolitan mobility. It launched numerous electric buses and cars. It was founded in China and has become a global leader in producing electric vehicles.

The company has begun to contribute significantly to cleaner environments and enhanced public health. BYD's electric buses are a significant advancement in reducing air pollution. A 2023 study by the International Council on Clean Transportation (ICCT) analyzed the impact of BYD's electric buses in major cities such as Shenzhen and Los Angeles.[244]

The study found that the deployment of BYD's electric buses resulted in a noticeable reduction in air pollution, which also decreased nitrogen oxide (NOx) and particulate matter (PM2.5) in the air.

This improvement in air quality is particularly significant in densely populated urban areas where traditional diesel

---

[244]https://theicct.org/wp-content/uploads/2023/12/ID-57-%E2%80%93-ZETs-China_Final.pdf

buses have been primary sources of air pollution. The environmental benefits of BYD's electric buses also come with economic advantages.

A 2022 report from the National Renewable Energy Laboratory (NREL) indicated that the total cost of ownership for BYD's electric buses is lower than that of conventional diesel buses. [245] [246] This cost efficiency is due to lower fuel and maintenance expenses.

At the same time, electric buses with dramatically fewer moving parts and less frequent need for maintenance offer a more economical alternative for private and public transportation agencies. Both companies have shown how embracing sustainable practices can drive positive environmental and economic outcomes. Tesla's leadership in electric vehicles and renewable energy integration has set a high standard for the automotive industry. On the other hand, BYD's innovations in electric buses demonstrate the potential for cleaner and sustainable passenger transportation.

These case studies highlight the benefits of adopting sustainability as a core principle and provide valuable insights for other organizations looking to integrate environmentally friendly practices into their operations.

This shift toward sustainability in passenger transportation is an opportunity for economic growth and competitive advantage. As more companies and startups follow the lead

---

[245]https://www.nrel.gov/docs/fy23osti/83232.pdf
[246]https://ieahev.org/wp-content/uploads/2022/05/digital hevtcp_2022_annual_report_final-with-cover-1.pdf

of Tesla and BYD, the mobility industry will continue to evolve toward a more sustainable and abundant future

The Moving Wheel of Continuous Innovation in Passenger Transportation

Continuous innovation is more than a strategy for passenger transportation —it's a necessity. In a sector that is influenced by rapid technological advancements and shifting consumer expectations, the ability to innovate continuously can determine a company's market position and long-term success. It's entrepreneurship fundamentals.

Innovation helps companies stay competitive by introducing new products or improving existing services. It often refers to responding to emerging trends in the respective market or industry. This constant evolution is crucial for staying ahead of competitors.

Take Waymo, for example. It is slowly becoming a trendsetter in autonomous vehicle technology. It started as a Google Self-Driving Car Project but has become a pioneer in developing self-driving technology. The company's innovations include developing advanced sensor systems, machine learning algorithms, and simulation platforms.[247] All of that enables vehicles to navigate complex urban environments with high precision.[248]

---

[247]https://www.wevolver.com/article/2023-autonomous-vehicle-report/tech-stack

[248]https://fortune.com/2024/05/29/waymo-self-driving-robo-taxi-uber-tesla-alphabet/

Waymo's vehicles are equipped with a suite of sensors like lidar, radar, and cameras, which provide a comprehensive 360-degree view of their surroundings.[249] These sensors feed data into Waymo's proprietary software, which uses machine learning to interpret the data and make real-time driving decisions. As mentioned in earlier chapters, this technology has undergone extensive testing, including millions of miles driven on public roads and billions of miles in simulation.

Another notable example is May Mobility, which has made strides in microtransit with autonomous vehicles. The company's pilot programs in cities like Grand Rapids and Ann Arbor showcase how microtransit solutions can provide flexible, on-demand transportation while integrating seamlessly with existing public transit systems.

A 2024 report by Fortune Business Insights indicated that the autonomous vehicle market could reach $13,632 billion by 2030.[250] With that in mind, it is easy to understand how May Mobility's and Waymo's technology disrupts traditional transportation models. It will reduce the need for personal car ownership and change metropolitan mobility in the long run.

Furthermore, a study reports that the autonomous vehicle market is estimated at $2 trillion in 2023 and could grow at a compound annual growth rate (CAGR) of 13.5%

---

[249]https://downloads.ctfassets.net/sv23gofxcuiz/4gZ7ZUxd4SRj1D1W6z3r pR/2ea16814cdb42f9e8eb34cae4f30b35d/2021-03-waymo-safety-report.pdf

[250] https://www.fortunebusinessinsights.com/autonomous-vehicle-market-109045

from 2024 to 2032.[251] The main reasons behind these advancements include technology, regulatory support, and increased investment in R&D.[252]

Autonomous vehicles (AVs) are essential to creating a future defined by abundant mobility. By significantly reducing the cost per mile—from an average of $2.50 to $3.00 for traditional ride-hailing services down to a projected $0.50 to $1.00 with AV technology—they are reshaping affordability and access in transportation. Additionally, traditional vehicles typically have a utilization rate of around 5%, while AVs are projected to achieve utilization rates as high as 70%, maximizing operational efficiency and resource usage.

Furthermore, maintenance costs are expected to decrease by 20% due to the streamlined mechanics and reduced wear and tear inherent in AV technology. Together, these advancements pave the way for a more democratic, inclusive, and equitable mobility industry, fostering an abundant future where transportation is accessible and affordable for all.[253]

---

[251] https://www.gminsights.com/industry-analysis/autonomous-vehicle-market

[252] https://www.bcg.com/publications/2022/update-on-shared-autonomous-electric-vehicles-market

[253] Makahleh, H. Y., Ferranti, E. J. S., & Dissanayake, D. (2024). Assessing the role of autonomous vehicles in urban areas: A systematic review of literature. *Future Transportation,* 4(2), 321–348. https://doi.org/10.3390/futuretransp4020017

Innovative Business Models and Service Integration

Innovative business models have been essential in helping companies adapt to changing market conditions and consumer preferences. Subscription models and shared mobility solutions are the perfect example of these issues. These models address the growing demand for flexible and cost-effective transportation options. Moreover, they also align with the increasing trends toward sustainability and reduced car ownership.

For example, TNCs continuously evolved their business model to stay relevant and competitive. Initially, they launched as a simple ride-hailing app. However, it later expanded its services to include various transportation options such as shared rides, food delivery, and trucking logistics. This diversification showed how TNCs were strategizing to integrate multiple services into a single platform. As a result, this provided users with a seamless transportation experience.

TNCs also invested heavily in developing algorithms for dynamic pricing, route optimization, and driver-partner matching. Additionally, Uber and Lyft have explored autonomous vehicle technology through partnerships with companies like Waymo and May Mobility.[254] These integrations of technology enhances operational efficiency and customer experience.

---

[254]https://www.statista.com/statistics/1156066/leading-ride-hailing-operators-worldwide-by-market-share/

Market analysis reports like those from Statista and PwC also illustrate the impact of Uber's business model on the mobility industry. Statista reported that Uber was the market leader, with a 25% share of the global ride-hailing market in 2022.[255] In addition, a report by McKinsey indicated that shared mobility could generate nearly $1 trillion in consumer spending by 2030.[256]

Scalability Through Strategic Partnerships

The passenger transportation sector has also adopted efficient scalability models. The growing innovation has helped companies expand and adapt to changing market conditions. This also includes increasing or decreasing service offerings based on demand fluctuations.

Companies can do that without compromising quality or efficiency. In doing so, many companies have made abundant models the core components of their operations.

Tesla's Supercharger network is a prime example of how strategic partnerships and scalability can drive success.[257] It was launched in 2012 as a network to support long-distance electric vehicle travel by providing high-speed charging

---

[255] Statista. (2022). *Leading ride-hailing operators worldwide by market share*. Retrieved from https://www.statista.com

[256]https://www.mckinsey.com/industries/automotive-and-assembly/our-insights/shared-mobility-sustainable-cities-shared-destinies#:~:text=By%202030%2C%20shared%20mobility%20could%20gener ate%20up%20to%20%241%20trillion%20in%20consumer%20spending.%20N ew%20research%20reveals%20the%20trends%20and%20data%20to%20know

[257]https://ir.tesla.com/press-release/tesla-motors-launches-revolutionary-supercharger-enabling

stations across strategic locations.[258] This network is crucial for overcoming range anxiety and making electric vehicles suitable for more drivers.

In 2023, Tesla operates over 40,000 Superchargers globally.[259] It has stations in more than 40 countries. The expansion of this network was possible due to collaborations with property owners, businesses, and municipalities. As a result, it allowed the installation of charging stations at convenient locations such as shopping centers and highway rest stops.

According to Tesla's 2023 Impact Report, the Supercharger network has significantly contributed to the company's growth.[260] The report notes that Supercharger usage has increased year-on-year, showing the growing adoption of Tesla vehicles. Furthermore, it also gives evidence of the network's effectiveness in reducing charging times.

BYD also successfully launched strategic partnerships to improve the scalability of its products. The company formed alliances with various cities and transportation agencies to deploy electric buses and trucks. These partnerships have helped the company enhance its market presence and promote adopting electric transportation solutions.

---

[258]https://energyx.com/blog/electrifying-the-drive-tesla-supercharger-network-and-the-ev-revolution/

[259]https://www.businessinsider.com/tesla-supercharger-network-electric-vehicle-charging-infrastructure-gm-mercedes-2023-1

[260]https://www.tesla.com/ns_videos/2023-tesla-impact-report-highlights.pdf

One example is BYD's partnership with the city of Los Angeles. The company supplied a fleet of electric buses for public transit to the city.[261] This partnership showed BYD's commitment to supporting sustainable mobility while addressing the challenges of air pollution and congestion.

A 2023 report by Bloomberg (BNEF) indicates that BYD has delivered over 80,000 electric buses.[262] As a result, it was one of the largest suppliers of electric buses worldwide.[263]

Microtransit solutions further illustrate effective scalability. For instance, May Mobility's deployment of autonomous vehicles, using a platform of special factory design model of Toyota's Sienna hybrid cars are used for on-demand transportation in Ann Arbor, Grand Rapids and Miami, highlight how strategic partnerships and adaptable service models can meet varying urban transportation needs.

The Growing Shift Toward Consumer-Centric Approaches

Businesses have shifted their focus from merely offering products and services to truly understanding and addressing consumer needs and preferences. This involves tailoring products to meet specific demands and enhancing overall user experiences to foster satisfaction and loyalty. For

---

[261]https://www.energy.ca.gov/sites/default/files/2024-03/CEC-600-2024-013.pdf
[262]https://cnevpost.com/2024/07/04/byd-secures-bus-order-azerbaijan/
[263]https://www.byd.com/za/news-list/south-africa-electric-bus-deal.html

companies in the mobility industry, this approach means prioritizing user-friendly features, reliable services, and personalized experiences.

Businesses can drive growth and differentiate themselves from competitors by placing the consumer at the center of innovation. However, they must understand consumer behaviors, preferences, and pain points. This will enable companies to design solutions that resonate with their target audience and deliver value beyond basic functionality.

Google also showed a consumer-centric approach through its continuous innovation to improve user experience. From its search engine to products like Google Maps and Google Assistant, the company prioritizes user needs and feedback to enhance functionality and usability.

One notable example is Google Maps. It involved improvements based on user input. The app offers real-time traffic updates, turn-by-turn navigation, and local business information. All of that is designed to improve the user's travel experience. Google's focus on user-centric features like personalized recommendations and accurate route information. This has made Google Maps an indispensable tool for millions globally.

A February 2024 report by Statista indicates that Google Maps will be the leading mapping app in the United States in 2023. It had over 21 billion downloads.[264]

---

[264]https://www.statista.com/statistics/865413/most-popular-us-mapping-apps-ranked-by-audience/

Tesla has also embraced a consumer-centric approach. This was due to its focus on customer experience enhancements. The company's commitment to providing a seamless and personalized experience is noticeable in its direct-to-consumer sales model. It also offered over-the-air software updates and innovative features such as Autopilot.[265]

A 2013 report on Reuters stated that the Tesla Model S had the highest owner satisfaction rate.[266] This rating reflects positive feedback on vehicle performance, innovation, and customer service. Moreover, Tesla's annual surveys reveal high levels of customer loyalty. Many owners expressed a strong likelihood of recommending the brand to others.

What Are The Implications of Abundant Models?

The concept of abundant models is transforming the global economy and societal structures. These models are creating an environment of innovation, sustainability, and efficiency. The emphasis on sustainable transportation solutions like electric vehicles and shared mobility services is changing how people move and how transportation systems are integrated into economic frameworks.

This shift is not only reducing carbon footprints but also influencing economic structures. For instance, the rise of

---

[265]https://www.researchgate.net/publication/379555334_The_Innovations_Driving_Tesla's_Success_Disruptions_Competition_Business_Model_Customer_Transformation_and_Entrepreneurial_Strategies
[266]https://www.reuters.com/article/business/tesla-gets-top-marks-in-consumer-reports-satisfaction-survey-idUSL2N0J601E/

electric vehicles (EVs) impacts the oil industry and creates new opportunities for battery manufacturers and charging infrastructure providers.[267]

NextEra Energy is an exceptional example of how abundant models can transform the industry.[268] The company is one of the largest renewable energy providers in the world. It has significantly advanced the renewable energy sector through substantial wind and solar power investments.[269]

NextEra Energy generates over 45,000 megawatts of renewable energy capacity.[270] This makes it one of the largest wind and solar power producers globally. For example, in 2022 alone, the company added approximately 3,000 megawatts of renewable energy capacity.[271]

Global Shift Toward Sustainability and Innovation

The influence of abundant models is far beyond the passenger transportation sector. It is driving significant changes across various industries. It focuses on sustainability and innovation, which leads to developing business models that promote sustainable energy, and technological practices. In energy, for instance, the transition

---

[267]https://www.sciencedirect.com/science/article/pii/S2666202722000039

[268]https://www.nexteraenergy.com/content/dam/nee/us/en/pdf/2023_NEE_Sustainability_Report_Final.pdf

[269]https://www.nexteraenergy.com/content/dam/nee/us/en/pdf/2023_NEE_Sustainability_Report_Final.pdf

[270]https://www.investor.nexteraenergy.com/news-and-events/news-releases/2016/06-06-2016-201944903

[271]https://www.cnbc.com/2024/07/24/renewable-energy-demand-will-triple-as-electricity-consumption-surges-nextera-ceo-says.html

to renewable resources is not limited to transportation. It also impacts electricity generation, heating, and industrial processes.

Then innovations like smart grids and energy storage solutions have become more prevalent over the years. They enhance the efficiency and reliability of energy systems.

SpaceX is one of the best examples of how abundant models drive innovation and sustainability in sectors outside traditional industries. The company is focusing on making space exploration more affordable and sustainable. It has made advancements in space technology mainly due to its reusable rocket technology.

The Falcon 9 is designed to return to Earth and for reuse. This significantly reduces the cost of access to space.[272] The company's Starship program further bolsters this goal by creating a fully reusable spacecraft capable of carrying humans to Mars and beyond.

In 2015, SpaceX successfully landed the first stage of the Falcon 9 rocket back on Earth.[273] In 2023, SpaceX had completed over 200 successful launches.[274]

Cultivating Abundant Tribes within Transportation Providers' Organizations

[272]https://nstxl.org/reducing-the-cost-of-space-travel-with-reusable-launch-vehicles/#:~:text=The%20Falcon%209%20is%20a,the%20cost%20of%20space%20access

[273]https://www.theverge.com/2015/12/21/10640306/spacex-elon-musk-rocket-landing-success

[274]https://www.cnbc.com/2023/12/29/spacex-rockets-2023-launch-record.html

Developing abundant tribes within transportation providers' organizations is a cornerstone of adopting an abundant mindset. An abundant tribe is more than just a team or community—it embodies a shared ethos of growth, innovation, and sustainability. This mindset thrives in a collaborative environment that brings together diverse perspectives, fosters goals alignment and drives collective progress.

Consider the example of **RedCoach**, a private intercity bus transportation provider in the United States. RedCoach has successfully differentiated itself by fostering a culture of innovation and excellence, focusing on premium comfort and convenience for passengers while staying competitive in a challenging market. By creating an abundant tribe within their organization, RedCoach has empowered its teams to constantly seek new ways to enhance service offerings, optimize route efficiency, and embrace technology-driven solutions for an improved customer experience. This collaborative ethos has enabled RedCoach to adapt and thrive, offering reliable, high-quality transportation options and solidifying its place as a preferred choice for travelers seeking luxury and affordability in intercity transit.[285]

Passenger transportation providers must follow this path and foster abundant organizations by cultivating collaborative tribes within their ranks. These tribes become living embodiments of the provider's vision and model of abundance, infusing every initiative with purpose and driving collective success. The abundant mindset is not just about adopting new technologies but about empowering teams to collaborate, innovate, and grow together, creating a lasting legacy of abundance in mobility.

Adoption of Abundant KPIs

Adopting abundant KPIs in transportation providers' organizations demonstrates an abundant mindset by setting ambitious, attainable metrics that drive long-term success, innovation, sustainability, and scalability. In the U.S., an exemplary livery and coach provider that embodies this approach is **Greyhound Lines, Inc.**, a leader in long-distance bus transportation. Greyhound has received attention for its efforts to modernize its fleet, improve customer experiences, and drive sustainability within the transportation sector.[275]

Greyhound's KPIs focus on operational efficiency, customer satisfaction, and reducing its environmental impact. For instance, the company has invested in upgrading its fleet with newer, more fuel-efficient buses that offer reduced carbon emissions compared to older models. Media outlets have highlighted Greyhound's adoption of clean-diesel technology and other green initiatives as a reflection of its commitment to sustainability. This aligns with abundant KPIs aimed at minimizing environmental impact while enhancing operational performance.

---

[275]https://finance.yahoo.com/news/luxury-motorcoach-company-redcoach-launches-140000276.html

To improve customer experience and scalability, Greyhound has implemented digital ticketing solutions, real-time tracking systems, and Wi-Fi availability across its buses, enabling seamless and connected travel for its passengers. The company's focus on enhancing rider comfort and service reliability is driven by KPIs that prioritize customer satisfaction, reflected in various customer-centric innovations. Greyhound has also expanded its network to better serve underserved areas, increasing accessibility and connectivity for passengers across the U.S.[276]

By prioritizing ambitious KPIs centered on sustainability, scalability, and customer satisfaction, Greyhound demonstrates how an abundant mindset can drive transformation and growth within the livery and coach transportation sector.

Emerging Abundant Technologies and Innovation

It is the integration of state-of-the-art tools and innovation to make gains in efficiency, scalability, and customer experience. Embracing such technologies helps one stay ahead of the competitive race of any industry.

As discussed in Chapter 10, technology and innovation are catalysts for accelerating provider growth in the new post-digital economy. By leveraging advanced technologies and fostering a culture of continuous

---

[276]https://www.prnewswire.com/news-releases/greyhound-and-flixbus-combine-technology-to-create-the-largest-intercity-bus-network-enhancing-overall-traveler-experience-301757281.html

innovation, organizations can unlock new efficiencies and drive sustainability to enhance their competitive edge.

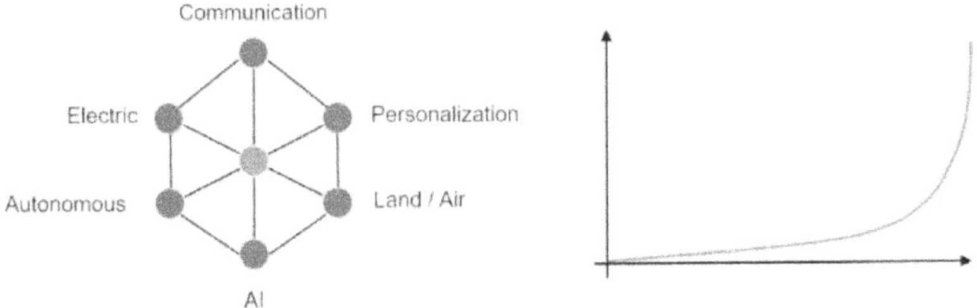

We have delved into the transformative impact within the passenger transportation sector, highlighting how embracing an abundant mindset and focusing on key dimensions can ignite a journey of exponential growth. By fostering innovation, collaboration, and sustainability, this industry can move toward an era of unparalleled opportunity.

However, amidst this promising landscape, it is critical to recognize the position and well-being of drivers—the indispensable stakeholders who power the passenger transportation sector. While their contributions are essential to this ecosystem, there remains a need to ensure they are not drawn in or harmed by the alluring, yet potentially damaging promises of dominant Transportation Network Companies (TNCs). The seductive appeal of flexible work schedules and on-demand income often obscures the reality of unstable wages, limited benefits, and eroded bargaining power that gig work can entail.

In the next chapter, we will closely examine the gig economy's broader dynamics and the profound impact it can have on drivers, communities, and the middle class at large. We will explore how an imbalanced ecosystem can exacerbate economic disparities, erode income stability, and ultimately impoverish the very workers it claims to empower. By uncovering the nuances and potential pitfalls of this gig-driven model, we can better understand how to foster a more equitable, balanced, and resilient system for all stakeholders involved.

Chapter 13
The Gig Economy's Hidden Cost: How It's Eroding the American Middle Class

"Work hard, learn, re-learn, and take control of your future in a rapidly changing world."

-Thomas Friedman

The gig economy includes short-term contracts, freelance work, and temporary positions. These are just a few examples of how the industry shifts from traditional employment models. Moving away from permanent and full-time jobs with defined benefits and long-term stability, gig work typically involves irregular hours, project-based tasks, and self-employment.

This model includes platforms like Uber, Lyft, Upwork, and Fiverr. They have proliferated across various sectors, from transportation to creative industries. The rise of the gig economy has been mainly due to advancements in technology and changes in consumer behavior.

Mobile apps and online platforms have facilitated a new labor market flexibility. They allowed workers to offer services directly to consumers without intermediaries. This model has democratized access to work opportunities and enabled individuals to earn income through short-term engagements and freelance projects.

McKinsey reported that nearly 58 million Americans were independent workers in 2022. This made up 36% of the employed respondents in a survey.[277] This shift has been due to various benefits like autonomy and flexibility in working conditions. However, this shift has also introduced several challenges.

Gig workers often lack traditional employment protections like health insurance, retirement benefits, and job security. This instability has numerous implications for economic stability, especially for the American middle class.

The shift from stable and full-time positions to gig-based work has contributed to the erosion of long-term financial security. As a result, it has raised concerns about the sustainability of the gig economy model and its impact on workers' well-being.

The rise of the Gig economy has overwhelmingly benefited the dominant software platforms, driving their profits higher at the expense of the workforce. A dangerous misconception has taken root: the idea that a Gig worker is an Entrepreneur. This is not only misleading but also harmful. A Gig worker is, in reality, a Self-Employed worker—a distinction with profound implications. These two roles are fundamentally different and should never have been conflated. The time to correct this misunderstanding is

---

[277]https://www.mckinsey.com/featured-insights/mckinsey-explainers/what-is-the-gig-economy

now before more lives are affected by this critical misrepresentation.

Gig Worker ≠ Entrepreneur

The Impact of the Gig Economy on the Passenger's Transportation Sector

The rise of ride-sharing platforms like Uber and Lyft seriously impacted the public mobility industry in metropolitan environments. They disrupted the conventional taxi services and established a new model of employment.

Before these platforms, taxi services were under a regulated framework with fixed pricing and licensing requirements. Drivers often worked for established taxi companies with the typical employment structure. It usually included fixed wages or commissions, regulated hours, and a more structured approach to job security and benefits.

Uber and Lyft introduced a decentralized model. In this model, individuals with a personal vehicle could become drivers and connect directly with passengers via mobile apps. It democratized the transportation sector and allowed for a more flexible and scalable system. A report by the Rideshare Guy stated that Uber had nearly 5.4 million drivers in 2022.[278] It showed the rapid adoption of gig-based driving jobs over the years.[279]

The growth of these platforms has had a serious impact on traditional taxi services and the livery sector. Those services have long struggled to compete with ride-sharing platforms' convenience and lower costs. Many cities have seen a decline in traditional taxi and livery services. Some companies went out of business or adapted their models to include app-based hailing services.[280] For instance, New York City's yellow taxi fleet saw a significant reduction in ridership and revenues. This happened while Uber and Lyft expanded their market share.[281]

The Concept of Job Security and Financial Stability

Ride-sharing platforms offer flexibility. However, they have significant drawbacks related to job security and financial stability. Gig workers like them experience substantial income variability. Their income is affected by factors like fluctuating demand, variable pricing, and platform algorithms.

These issues weren't commonplace with the roles of traditional employees. Moreover, gig workers do not have

---

[278] https://therideshareguy.com/uber-statistics/

[279] https://investor.uber.com/news-events/news/press-release-details/2023/Uber-Announces-Results-for-Fourth-Quarter-and-Full-Year-2022/default.aspx

[280] https://www.forbes.com/sites/michaelgoldstein/2018/06/08/uber-lyft-taxi-drivers/

[281] https://www.researchgate.net/publication/326745735_An_empirical_anal ysis_of_taxi_Lyft_and_Uber_rides_Evidence_from_weather_shocks_in_NYC

guaranteed hours or consistent income, which leads to financial uncertainty.

A comprehensive MIT Center for Energy and Environmental Policy Research analysis indicates that Uber drivers could earn a pretax profit median of around $3.37 after considering expenses.[282] This is below the average hourly wage for many full-time jobs and can vary depending on location, demand, and time of day. Further, reports confirm that many Uber drivers work part-time and rely on gig work as a supplementary income rather than a primary source of earnings.[283]

The lack of traditional employment benefits is also a critical issue. Uber drivers are gig workers, and like many of them, they also fall under the category of independent contractors. This means they are responsible for their health insurance, retirement savings, and other benefits. A national survey reported by Harvard University indicates that many gig workers have inadequate access to economic security and health benefits.[284]

Gig Drivers and Uber – A Close Inspection

A University of Illinois Urbana-Campaign report revealed that Uber drivers earned a gross income of around

---

[282] http://ceepr.mit.edu/files/papers/2018-005-Brief.pdf

[283] https://www.npr.org/sections/thetwo-way/2018/03/02/590168381/uber-lyft-drivers-earning-a-median-profit-of-3-37-per-hour-study-says

[284] https://shift.hks.harvard.edu/wp-content/uploads/2022/06/gig_brief.pdf

$23.23 per hour.[285] However, this figure drops when you start considering vehicle expenses and other operating costs. Moreover, the Economic Policy Institute found that Uber drivers could earn an equivalent of $9.21 in hourly wages.[286]

Job satisfaction among Uber drivers is also mixed. While some drivers appreciate the flexibility and independence of gig work, others report dissatisfaction due to financial instability and lack of benefits.[287] A 2019 Vox report found that many drivers were dissatisfied with their earnings.[288] In addition, many expressed concerns about the lack of job security and the difficulty of making a living wage.

The Nash Game Theory and Gig Work

Nash Game Theory was a concept by the US mathematician John Nash. He provided a helpful framework for understanding the dynamics of the gig economy. In this theory, the expert focuses on strategic decision-making in competitive environments where the outcome depends on the actions of multiple participants. In the context of the gig economy, Nash Game Theory can help explain why gig workers might face suboptimal outcomes despite their efforts to maximize their earnings.

---

[285]https://lep.illinois.edu/wp-content/uploads/2022/03/ILEPI-PMCR-Improving-Labor-Standards-for-Uber-and-Lyft-Drivers-FINAL.pdf
[286] https://www.epi.org/press/resources-research-uber-gig-economy/
[287]https://www.researchgate.net/publication/345435243_Uber_happy_Work_and_well-being_in_the_'Gig_Economy'
[288]https://www.vox.com/2019/5/8/18535367/uber-drivers-strike-2019-cities

You see, in a Nash equilibrium, each participant's strategy is optimal given the strategies of others. Hence, no one can benefit by changing their strategy alone. When you apply that to the gig economy, this theory suggests that individual gig workers, since they are acting in their self-interest, may accept lower wages or substandard working conditions because they believe this is the best they can achieve.

However, this is in a competitive environment of platform algorithms and policies. This results in a scenario where, even if all workers would benefit from higher pay and better conditions, no single worker has an incentive to reject low-paying gigs because others will not do the same.

Arguably, the gig economy creates a race to the bottom regarding wages and working conditions.[289] This is mainly due to the high worker competition and the lack of collective bargaining power.[290] It also highlights that the competitive nature of gig work often leads to a downward spiral in earnings and job quality. Hence, the Nash equilibrium is where workers continue to accept less favorable terms.

---

[289] https://journals.sagepub.com/doi/10.1177/0308518X19894584
[290]https://www.researchgate.net/publication/351235960_The_Ethical_Deba te_About_the_Gig_Economy_A_Review_and_Critical_Analysis

Worldwide Perspective and Response to the Impact of the Gig Economy

The gig economy has evolved differently across various countries over the years. There have been significant differences in regulatory, cultural, and economic contexts. In developed economies like the United States and the UK, gig work has often been characterized by its flexibility and lack of stability.[291] Conversely, gig work can provide crucial income opportunities without robust formal employment sectors in emerging economies.[292]

In the UK, ride-sharing and delivery platforms have been facing intense scrutiny.[293] Deliveroo is a leading food delivery service central to numerous controversies regarding worker rights.[294] Recent reports reveal that Deliveroo has faced legal challenges over its employment practices. In 2021, a UK employment tribunal ruled that Deliveroo's delivery riders are not entitled to employee status and benefits like minimum wage and paid leave.[295]

This contradicted the company's claims that its riders are independent contractors. This decision has sparked ongoing debates about workers' rights and has led to stronger protections for gig workers. Moreover, advocacy groups

---

[291] https://sdgsreview.org/LifestyleJournal/article/download/1605/1478/4782

[292] https://link.springer.com/chapter/10.1007/978-3-031-59944-6_8

[293] https://www.loc.gov/item/global-legal-monitor/2017-09-29/england-uber-faces-legal-challenges-and-scrutiny/

[294] https://www.bbc.com/news/business-56510493

[295] https://www.thegrocer.co.uk/technology-and-supply-chain/deliveroo-riders-are-not-employees-rules-supreme-court/685617.article

pushed for regulatory changes to ensure fair treatment and benefits.

In Spain, there has been significant legislative progress to improve the conditions of gig workers. In 2021, Spain enacted a landmark labor reform that classifies certain gig economy workers, especially delivery riders, as employees rather than independent contractors.[296]

This new classification mandates that these workers receive benefits such as paid sick leave, unemployment insurance, and job security. The law came to be known as the "Riders Law."[297] It showed a growing recognition of the need to adapt labor regulations to modern work arrangements. Furthermore, it has been closely supervised by other countries that are considering similar reforms.

The expansion of the gig economy has implications for job security and the traditional middle-class models. It has disrupted the conventional employment model, defined as stable jobs. These jobs under that model had benefits like health insurance and retirement plans. In its place, many gig workers face income instability and a lack of essential protections.

The Economic Policy Institute indicates that gig workers experience greater income volatility.[298] The findings also suggest that these workers face significant financial

---

[296]https://gigpedia.org/resources/visuals/2023/being-a-gig-worker-in-spain-jun-2023

[297]https://industrialrelationsnews.ioe-emp.org/industrial-relations-and-labour-law-may-2021/news/article/spain-approves-a-riders-law

[298]https://www.epi.org/publication/gig-worker-survey/

uncertainty, and many struggle to maintain a consistent income. Data shows that many gig workers report having a low income. Moreover, many earn below the national minimum wage when accounting for expenses like vehicle amortization maintenance and fuel.[299]

The Path Forward - Addressing Challenges and Proposing Solutions

Innovative policy solutions can be a significant step forward in addressing the challenges faced by gig workers. One proposed solution is the introduction of portable benefits. This would allow gig workers to retain benefits such as health insurance and retirement savings across different jobs and platforms. This approach will also provide workers with a safety net similar to traditional employment while retaining the flexibility of gig work.

Policy Think Tanks like the Urban Institute have explored the impact of portable benefits. It found that such systems could provide crucial financial security for gig workers. A report by the Urban Institute indicates that portable benefits could significantly improve financial stability and health outcomes for gig workers.[300] It would offer continuous access to essential services regardless of employment status.

---

[299]https://www.epi.org/publication/gig-worker-survey/
[300]https://www.urban.org/sites/default/files/2023-04/A-convening-on-reimagining-social-protections-for-independent-and-other-traditionally-excluded-workers-final.pdf

Additionally, minimum wage guarantees can ensure fair and livable income for all gig workers. Nevertheless, implementing minimum wage standards will be important in mitigating the income instability these gig workers face. Moreover, it will provide a baseline level of earnings and reduce the financial pressures of gig work.

On the other hand, companies can adopt fair labor practices and set new standards in the gig economy. **Alto**, a ride-hailing service, has taken a different approach by hiring drivers as employees rather than independent contractors.[301] This model provides drivers job security, health insurance, and other benefits. It is remarkably different from the previously novel gig economy practices where drivers were independent contractors with limited access to benefits.

Going forward, private providers must adhere to fair and sustainable practices in the evolving gig economy. They must practice investments in worker training, career advancement opportunities, and competitive wages. That could enhance worker satisfaction and contribute to long-term business success.

Research from Harvard Business Review indicates that businesses prioritizing ethical practices and investing in their workforce see improved performance and employee retention.[302] Investing in employee training and development can potentially lead to greater operational

---

[301]https://www.nytimes.com/2023/10/05/business/alto-uber-drivers-alternative.html
[302]https://hbr.org/2022/07/its-time-to-reimagine-employee-retention

efficiency.[303] In turn, that could drive higher levels of customer satisfaction and demonstrate the benefits of a long-term, worker-centered approach.

Moreover, developing innovative worker protections like portable benefits can also serve as a model for the gig economy. Starbucks' provision of comprehensive benefits to part-time employees shows that businesses can support their workforce beyond traditional full-time employment models.[304]

Promoting Ethical Employment and Economic Stability

Amtrak, the National Railroad Passenger Corporation, is a notable example of achieving significant improvements in operational efficiency and worker satisfaction through investment in employee development.[305] The company has committed to comprehensive training programs to enhance the skills of its workforce and provide career advancement opportunities.

This investment includes extensive training programs, leadership development initiatives, and career progression paths. According to Amtrak's annual reports, the company spends millions annually on training and development.[306]

---

[303]https://core.ac.uk/download/pdf/234624593.pdf

[304]https://www.researchgate.net/publication/342916687_Starbucks'_Human_Resource_Management_Practices

[305]https://www.washingtonpost.com/transportation/2022/06/02/amtrak-expansion-workforce/

[306]https://www.amtrakoig.gov/sites/default/files/reports/Training%20Eval%20Report%20Final.pdf

Furthermore, the evolving nature of work in the gig economy has encouraged many companies to innovate outside traditional employment models. This includes offering comprehensive benefits that address the unique needs of modern workers. Companies like Starbucks have provided robust benefits packages far beyond the standard offerings.

The company gained attention for its inclusive benefits package, which extended to part-time employees—a notable deviation from traditional practices where such benefits are reserved for full-time staff.[304] Studies have shown that such benefits contribute to a more stable and motivated workforce.[307]

Importance of Participatory Work Environments

When businesses create collaborative work environments where employees have a say in decision-making processes, it can lead to higher job satisfaction and positive workplace cultures. This is called the participatory work environment, where business leaders encourage open communication and empower employees to promote a sense of ownership and engagement.

Research indicates that organizations with participatory management practices experience higher innovation and job satisfaction.[308] When employees participate in decision-

---

[307] https://www.atlantis-press.com/article/125908470.pdf
[308]https://www.researchgate.net/publication/343057415_participatory_man agement_and_employee_satisfactionrevised-1-1_ugwu_et_al_2020

making and have a voice in shaping their work conditions, they are more likely to feel motivated and committed to their roles. This collaborative approach boosts morale and drives organizational success.[309]

Semco Partners adopted corporate democracy to transform workplace dynamics and drive success.[310] Under the leadership of Ricardo Semler, Semco adopted a radical approach to management. It allowed employees significant control over their work conditions and company decisions.[311]

The company's model included self-managed teams, flexible work hours, and transparency in decision-making processes. [312] Employees have a say in critical aspects of the business. Surprisingly, this includes hiring, salary levels, and company policies. This approach resulted in high levels of innovation, employee satisfaction, and organizational resilience.

For those reasons, ethical employment practices and economic stability in the gig economy still require a multi-step approach. Companies like Amtrak and Starbucks share evidence of how investment in employee development and comprehensive benefits can create a more stable and

---

[309]https://www.ncbi.nlm.nih.gov/pmc/articles/PMC9136218/

[310]https://ivypanda.com/essays/ricardo-semlers-leadership-at-semco-partners/

[311]https://threecontinentcourseforthewickedandbrave.files.wordpress.com/2014/02/final-semco-group.pdf

[312]https://www.researchgate.net/publication/335928164_Democratic_work places_and_its_linkages_to_new_and_sustainable_business_models_The_case _of_Semco_SA_Journal_Accountancy_Business

motivated workforce. At the same time, Semco Partners also showed the benefits of a participatory work environment that encourages collaboration and innovation.

However, the gig economy is evolving continuously. It adopts ethical practices and focuses on long-term worker welfare, potentially leading to a more equitable and sustainable economic landscape.

As we explored in this chapter, the downside of the gig economy in the Post-Digital Economy Model reveals how the American middle class has faced increasing economic challenges, especially as labor structures shift and traditional safety nets weaken. For passenger transportation providers, however, the transformation within the mobility industry presents a paramount opportunity to thrive in this evolving landscape. By embracing new digital dimensions—such as streamlined operations, enhanced customer experiences, and data-driven decision-making—providers have a unique chance to redefine their roles and succeed in ways that past gig models failed to deliver.

Yet, transformation requires a clear strategy. Like any entrepreneur or provider seeking to ride this new wave of innovation, navigating without understanding the forces at play can be perilous. Surfing without studying the tides is a risky business. To ensure success, we must first delve into the economic implications and actionable solutions that will empower stakeholders to conquer this new frontier. By examining these factors, we can better understand how to seize opportunities, overcome challenges, and reshape the industry into one that uplifts both businesses and workers for a more equitable ecosystem.

242

Chapter 14
Economic Implications:
How Shifting Markets Are
Shaping Our Future

The passenger transportation sector has substantially transformed over the past decade. It evolved from traditional taxi and livery services to a dynamic industry with diverse ride-hailing platforms and mobility solutions.

This industry, once defined predominantly by regulated taxis and livery, now includes a broad spectrum of services, including ride-sharing apps. It also featured car rental services, bike-sharing programs, and, more recently, Mobility as a Service (MaaS) platforms.

This evolution has shown broader consumer behavior and technology shifts within the mobility industry. It has significantly transformed how people move within metropolitan and rural environments, and influenced numerous economic and social factors.

The economic implications of these shifts have been the subject of studies and analysis for numerous reasons. The first is how these changes have impacted employment models and job creation within the industry. The growing changes affected how workers in the sector interacted with worker benefits. Furthermore, it also had a noticeable implication on the overall economic stability of the industry.

The gig-based employment model became prevalent in many modern passenger transportation services, introducing opportunities and challenges. While these models offered flexible income options and democratized access to transportation, they also raised concerns about job security and income variability. As discussed in the previous chapter, it also led to the erosion of traditional employment benefits.

When we examine the broader economic impact of the passenger transportation sector, we see that it significantly influenced local economies. It also had a significant impact on community well-being. For example, ride-hailing and microtransit services have led to changes in traffic patterns, urban planning, local business interactions, inclusion and equity.

Passenger transportation providers have started experimenting with new business models and technologies like those integrating Mobility as a Service (MaaS) and other innovative solutions. Through these changes, the implications for job quality and economic equity have become increasingly evident.

The Rise of Ride-Hailing Applications and Mobile Platforms

We often mark the rise of ride-hailing platforms with names like Uber and Lyft, and it is fair. These platforms revolutionized transportation and offered a modern alternative to traditional livery and taxi services. The companies were launched in 2009 and 2012, respectively.

The platforms used smartphone technology to provide on-demand transportation, significantly altering how people moved across cities.[313] For instance, users can request a ride via mobile apps, track their driver in real-time, pay seamlessly through the platform, and even share live locations for in-commute security. That has introduced unprecedented convenience and flexibility in urban mobility for commuters.[314]

Uber and Lyft have expanded rapidly over the last decade in terms of geographical reach and user base.[315] A study indicated that the platform had 118 million monthly active users globally, an average of around 19 million daily trips.[316] The study reports that the company recorded a 71% market share for ride-sharing and a 27% market share for food delivery services.

On the other hand, Lyft reported nearly 22.4 million active riders in the United States in the Fourth Quarter of 2023 despite being relatively smaller than Uber.[317] These platforms have had a major impact on urban transportation as a cost-effective and efficient alternative to traditional taxis.

A 2023 study by the International Transport Forum indicates that the rise of ride-hailing services and

---

[313]https://www.sciencedirect.com/science/article/abs/pii/S2543000918300106

[314] https://stride.ce.ufl.edu/wp-content/uploads/sites/153/2020/06/STRIDE-Project-B-Final-Report.pdf

[315]https://www.sciencedirect.com/science/article/abs/pii/S0094119020300899

[316]https://thesis.unipd.it/retrieve/c1ffa383-4a47-42df-9307-be1cadf42545/Frassetto_Marisa.pdf

[317]https://www.statista.com/statistics/916456/lyft-number-of-rides/

mode-shifts has been influential in helping economies achieve sustainability goals with environmentally-friendly initiatives.[318]

Comparative Analysis of Traditional Taxis and Livery vs. Ride-Hailing Services

Ride-hailing platforms disrupted the traditional taxi and livery sectors by offering more competitive pricing. They provided greater convenience and enhanced user experience than conventional taxis and livery. The traditional taxis and livery were often regulated and required pre-scheduled rides or street hails.

This led to the taxi and livery services facing challenges in matching ride-hailing services' on-demand, app-based convenience. The disruption was evident initially, but using various metrics like market share and financial performance made it more apparent for analysts and industry experts.

In New York City, for instance, the number of traditional yellow cabs has been declining since the introduction of ride-hailing services.[319] The revenue of conventional taxi services has also been impacted.[320] The National Bureau of Economic Research claims that the entry of Uber and Lyft also impacted taxi revenues in major U.S. cities while reducing the barriers to entry into the market.[321]

---

[318]https://www.itf-oecd.org/sites/default/files/docs/itf-transport-outlook-2023-launch.pdf

[319]https://www.sciencedirect.com/science/article/abs/pii/S0968090X21002485

[320]https://www.sciencedirect.com/science/article/abs/pii/S2210670722002463

[321]https://www.nber.org/system/files/working_papers/w23891/w23891.pdf

Analysis of How Ride-Hailing Provides Income Flexibility for Drivers

One of the key attractions of ride-hailing platforms is the flexibility they offer drivers. The traditional employment model involved fixed hours and locations. However, the ride-hailing drivers can choose when and where they work. This flexibility particularly appeals to individuals seeking supplementary income or those unable to commit to a traditional 9-to-5 job.

Uber and Lyft have diverse driver demographics. They include various age groups, socioeconomic backgrounds, and employment statuses.[322] Uber has around drivers between the ages of 25 and 54 and many of them are from minority groups.[323] Lyft's 2023 driver survey found similar trends, with a substantial portion of drivers using the platform as a secondary source of income.[324]

However, driver earnings have been a point of contention.[325] A study found that while many drivers appreciate the flexibility, they often face financial instability

---

[322]https://omswww.files.svdcdn.com/production/downloads/academic/Uber _Drivers_of_Disruption.pdf

[323]https://www.trtworld.com/magazine/the-pakistan-origin-driver-behind-a-landmark-uber-case-41040

[324]https://www.lyft.com/blog/posts/2023-economic-impact-report

[325]https://www.nytimes.com/2020/07/12/business/economy/uber-lyft-drivers-wages.html

due to fluctuating demand,[326] high operational costs, and platform fees.[327]

A 2018 report found that Uber drivers could make around $8.55 per hour or less. It indicated that the median hourly profit was around $10.[328] Moreover, there was a concern about driver wages in Minneapolis, which led to serious tension between the city council and Uber and Lyft.[329]

Stability vs Flexibility in the Passenger Transportation Sector

Numerous companies in the mobility industry are experimenting with business models to offer more traditional employment benefits compared to the gig economy's standard practices. Two notable examples are Allygator Shuttle and Bolt (formerly Taxify). These companies tried to blend the flexibility of ride-hailing with the security of traditional employment.

Allygator Shuttle is based in Berlin and operates with a model that emphasizes stability for its drivers. Dissimilar to how the gig economy platforms work, where drivers are classified as independent contractors, Allygator Shuttle provides its drivers with full-time employment status.

---

[326] https://www.reuters.com/article/world/mit-study-that-found-low-pay-for-uber-drivers-to-be-revisited-idUSKCN1GF0RM/

[327] https://www.nber.org/system/files/working_papers/w23296/w23296.pdf

[328] https://www.theguardian.com/technology/2018/mar/01/uber-lyft-driver-wages-median-report

[329] https://www.npr.org/2024/03/15/1238885721/uber-lyft-minneapolis-minimum-wage-law

This allows them to offer benefits like health insurance, paid leave, and other benefits such as pension contributions. A study indicated that Allygator Shuttle's employment model helped the company retain higher driver retention rates and improved job satisfaction compared to gig-based models.[330]

We also have Bolt, which is a ride-hailing platform originating from Estonia.[331] Bolt's model includes guaranteed minimum earnings, which help mitigate income volatility for drivers.[332] Additionally, Bolt offers a benefits package that includes health insurance and access to retirement savings plans in specific markets.[333]

An In-Depth Analysis of Traditional vs. Gig-Based Employment

As we explored in previous chapters the gig economy is characterized by short-term contracts and freelance work, which provides significant flexibility for workers but at the cost of job security and benefits. In contrast, companies like Allygator Shuttle and Bolt attempt to address these gaps by offering more stable employment arrangements while retaining flexibility.

---

[330]https://www.researchgate.net/publication/337737235_Introducing_a_Mobility_on_Demand_System_to_Prospective_Users_With_the_Help_of_a_Serious_Game

[331]https://www.bloomberg.com/news/articles/2023-12-20/uber-bolt-agree-to-pay-higher-wages-in-france-ahead-of-eu-rules

[332]https://www.ft.com/content/c7949a70-b4b6-45e1-9055-04c9aaaddc6a

[333]https://www.cityam.com/bolt-drivers-to-be-guaranteed-national-living-wage-while-remaining-self-employed/

Economic research highlights that stable employment models, such as those employed by Allygator Shuttle and Bolt, contribute to greater financial stability for workers. It is known that workers with access to benefits and job security are more likely to experience lower levels of economic stress and higher levels of job satisfaction.

This is because stable employment models can reduce the economic volatility associated with gig work. Moreover, it provides workers with a more predictable income and better long-term financial planning capabilities.

Regarding worker satisfaction, traditional employment models often score higher due to the security and benefits they provide.[334] A scientific study observed higher levels of anxiety and stress among self-employed individuals like gig workers in the passenger transportation sector, for example. The study highlighted the importance of non-monetary benefits in determining the welfare of workers in the gig economy.[335]

The Birth of Mobility as a Service (MaaS)

Mobility as a Service (MaaS) represented a transformative approach to metropolitan and rural transportation. It integrated various transportation modes into a unified service platform. MaaS platforms aim to streamline mobility by offering users a single interface to access public transit,

---

[334]https://www.researchgate.net/publication/341656571_Employees'_Job_Satisf action_and_their_Work_Performance_as_Elements_Influencing_Work_Safety

[335]https://www.researchgate.net/publication/345435243_Uber_happy_Wor k_and_well-being_in_the_'Gig_Economy'

ride-hailing, bike-sharing, car rentals, and other mobility services. This integration provides users with a more flexible and efficient way to navigate cities. Moreover, it potentially reduces the need for private vehicle ownership.

What are MaaS Platforms?

MaaS platforms are designed to offer comprehensive and seamless transportation solutions. Their key features include unified access, which allows users to access multiple transportation services through a single app or platform.[336]

Another feature includes real-time information through which users get live updates on schedules, traffic conditions, and availability. Furthermore, a MaaS platform allows users to pay for all transportation services through a single payment system. Moreover, these platforms offer customized travel suggestions based on user preferences and historical data.

One prominent example of a MaaS platform is Moovit, which we have also studied in the previous chapters. It is a global leader in public transit solutions. Moovit integrates various transportation modes, like buses, trains, ride-hailing services, and bike-sharing, into one accessible app. The company released a press release claiming that Moovit has over 950 million users worldwide in more than 3,400 cities across 112 countries.[337]

---

[336]https://www.mdpi.com/2071-1050/13/7/3666
[337]https://moovit.com/press-releases/2020-global-public-transport-report/

Case Study — MAGIIS

MAGIIS is another notable example of an AI powered MaaS platform. The company boasts advanced features and innovations to enhance providers' transportation services. It is focused on integrating various transportation models into a cohesive service offering, with features like autonomous dispatching, which utilizes AI to optimize ride assignments and reduce wait times.

Furthermore, the company's integrated payment processing feature simplifies transactions across different transportation modes and streamlines the providers' back-office operations. Moreover, the platform offers real-time assistance and updates to drivers while providing precise vehicle tracking to improve service reliability.

Its autonomous and open marketplace creates an "Always Available Experience" for passengers, allowing providers to share their cars autonomously to fulfill a passenger ride within the platform with open external vehicle ecosystems.

MAGIIS, with its 100% native-cloud platform, reported a 20% increase in sales for customers and a productivity increase of 40%. The company reported a turnover that increased by 500%.[338]

MAGIIS's vision is to empower and elevate passenger transportation providers on a global scale. By equipping entrepreneurs and providers to thrive in the emerging post-digital economy, MAGIIS seeks to create an inclusive and

---

[338]https://cloud.google.com/customers/magiis

equitable environment for all ecosystem stakeholders. This includes passengers, drivers, communities, government entities, technology providers, and complementary service providers. When everyone in the ecosystem is empowered, collaboration flourishes, innovation accelerates, and every participant can benefit from shared growth and success in a truly interconnected mobility landscape.

The Future of MaaS and Emergence of Situational Mobility

Situational Mobility is a concept where transportation solutions are tailored to specific user needs and contexts. MaaS platforms are expected to drive this trend by offering personalized mobility solutions that adapt to various situations, such as commuting, leisure, or special events.

For instance, MaaS could enable users to request a luxury, autonomous vehicle for an evening out or a practical electric SUV for daily commutes. This shift from traditional vehicle ownership to situational mobility could significantly alter transportation norms.[339]

Research indicates that the rise of the MaaS concept could lead to a reduction in car dependency in urban centers.[340] This change is expected due to the growing preference for flexible, on-demand transportation solutions. These

---

[339]https://www.sciencedirect.com/science/article/pii/S0965856424000120
[340]https://www.researchgate.net/publication/378727243_Mobility-as-a-service_and_unsustainable_travel_behaviour_Exploring_MaaS'_car_ownership_and_public_transport_trip_replacement_side-effects

solutions cater to specific needs rather than owning a personal vehicle.

There could be increased integration of emerging technologies, such as autonomous vehicles and electric mobility, in MaaS in the coming years.[341] Several studies and research highlight the possibility of MaaS platforms incorporating autonomous vehicles for enhanced efficiency and reduced operational costs.[342] Additionally, the rise of MaaS solutions can potentially reduce urban transportation emissions in the future based on scientific research.[343]

One of the significant benefits of MaaS is its potential to reduce the number of privately owned vehicles. And that is why it has gained immense popularity as it can lead to decreased traffic congestion and lower carbon emissions. Furthermore, it can also reduce parking demands related to private vehicle ownership.

The economic benefits of MaaS are above and beyond mere environmental impacts. They can reduce the need for personal vehicle ownership and lower transportation costs for individuals. Research highlights that MaaS could reduce personal transportation expenses and lead to more sustainable travel behaviors.[344]

The Multiplier Effect of Quality Job Creation

---

[341]https://www.juniperresearch.com/resources/blog/autonomous-vehicles-within-maas/
[342]https://www.sciencedirect.com/science/article/pii/S0967070X2300032X
[343]https://www.sciencedirect.com/science/article/pii/S0967070X23002810
[344]https://www.sciencedirect.com/science/article/pii/S1369847820304654

Quality job creation is a powerful driver of economic growth through the rapidly evolving mobility industry, especially in local communities. When businesses invest in creating stable, well-paying jobs with benefits, the positive effects influence the immediate employment environment. This generates a broader economic ripple effect.

Stable employment opportunities increase disposable income for workers, who, in turn, spend more on goods and services within their communities. This increased consumer spending stimulates local businesses, from retail stores and restaurants to service providers. This cycle of expenditure and reinvestment creates a robust economic ecosystem where local companies thrive and contribute to overall community prosperity.

In a 2022 study by the Economic Policy Institute (EPI), every $1 million increase in wages a business pays leads to an additional $1.25 million in economic activity within the local economy.[345] This study highlights how higher wages contribute to increased consumer spending and support for local businesses and services. This creates a multiplier effect that boosts the initial investment in job creation.

Case Study — Robert Reich's Insights

In his influential work *"The Work of Nations: Preparing Ourselves for 21st Century Capitalism,"* Robert Reich explores the concept of economic prosperity and its

---

[345]https://www.epi.org/publication/inequalitys-drag-on-aggregate-demand/

relationship with consumer demand. Reich argues that ensuring broad-based economic prosperity is crucial for fairness and sustaining consumer demand, underpinning business success.

Reich's analysis emphasizes that economic policies and business practices that support widespread prosperity contribute to a more dynamic and resilient economy. He posits that when workers have access to quality jobs, their increased purchasing power drives consumer demand, stimulating economic activity and business growth.

Reich's insights are supported by various economic studies highlighting the multiplier effect of quality job creation. For instance, reports show how quality job creation interlinks economic development and local community prosperity.[346] The creation of quality jobs has a positive impact on local economies and generates a ripple effect that stimulates economic activity and supports community prosperity.

Emergence of Innovative Policy Solutions and Corporate Best Practices

As the gig economy expands, policymakers are also in the run to introduce innovative solutions to address the challenges facing gig workers. These challenges particularly relate to on-the-job benefits and wage security. Portable benefits and minimum wage guarantees are key proposals in

---

[346]https://www.oecd.org/content/dam/oecd/en/publications/reports/2023/03/job-creation-and-local-economic-development-2023_ab3b49a8/21db61c1-en.pdf

progress for enhancing the economic stability of gig workers and addressing the shortcomings of traditional gig-based employment models.

Portable benefits are a system where workers, regardless of their employment status, can carry their benefits from one job to another. This approach addresses the benefit gaps for gig workers who typically do not receive traditional employment benefits (health insurance, retirement plans, and so on). Portable benefits can include these benefits that are not tied to a single employer but are accessible across different jobs and employers.

Minimum wage guarantees for gig workers are another critical policy reform. They can potentially ensure that all gig economy workers receive a fair wage that meets basic living standards. These reforms can provide a safety net for gig workers facing significant income variability and uncertainty.

A report from the Aspen Institute highlights the potential impact of portable benefits on gig workers.[347] The report emphasizes that such benefits could improve job security and well-being by offering stability and reducing financial stress. In a similar report by the National Employment Law Project (NELP) in 2021, it supported minimum wage guarantees.[348]

---

[347]https://www.aspeninstitute.org/wp-content/uploads/2019/06/Designing-Portable-Benefits_June-2019_Aspen-Institute-Future-of-Work-Initiative.pdf

[348]https://www.nelp.org/record-number-of-cities-states-will-increase-minimum-wages-in-2022/

The report indicates that implementing minimum wage policies in gig work could lead to a potential increase in overall earnings for gig workers. Meanwhile, it can also contribute to reduced income inequality.

Companies with Fair Labor Practices

Corporate responsibility is a crucial aspect of ensuring fair treatment for workers in the gig economy. Companies that adopt ethical labor practices can enhance their reputation and contribute to the broader goal of economic equity and sustainability. Starbucks and Alto are good examples for analysis in this context.

Alto, a ride-hailing company based in the United States, has adopted a unique employment model. It provides drivers with benefits and job security.[349] The company treats its drivers as full-time employees and offers them benefits like health insurance, retirement plans, and paid time off. This model contrasts sharply with the gig economy norm, where drivers are often classified as independent contractors without access to such benefits.[350]

Similarly, Starbucks is another notable example of a company providing extensive employee benefits. These benefits include part-time workers who receive health insurance, stock options, and tuition assistance from the company. A Harvard Business Review also highlights the

[349] https://www.autonews.com/mobility-report/why-ride-hailing-firm-offers-w-2-employment

[350] https://www.nytimes.com/2023/10/05/business/alto-uber-drivers-alternative.html

responsible company culture at Starbucks and how it impacts relationships between the company and its employees.[351]

Potentially Effective Strategies for Fair and Sustainable Practices

Adopting fair and sustainable practices is a moral obligation and a strategic advantage for business owners. It involves implementing equitable practices to improve employee satisfaction, reduce turnover, and enhance the company's reputation.

Business owners can consider several strategies to promote fairness and sustainability within their organizations, such as implementing comprehensive benefits. These can include health insurance, retirement plans, and paid leaves. While those are the only benefits we've been repeating, numerous others include maternity-paternity leave, paid sabbaticals, training programs, wellness initiatives, etc.

It can potentially enhance employee satisfaction and loyalty to the company. Furthermore, this approach also aligns with the models adopted by Alto and Starbucks. In addition, companies can practice fair wages which means adopting minimum wage guarantees. This will ensure all employees receive a living wage, which is crucial for economic equity. Businesses should review their compensation structures and adjust them to meet or exceed living wage standards.

---

[351] https://hbr.org/2016/12/how-starbuckss-culture-brings-its-strategy-to-life

Moreover, creating inclusive work environments within the company can be a powerful tool for driving success and internal collaboration. Combined with the strategic changes in the mobility industry, organizations with inclusive work environments will be better suited to cater to diverse consumer needs.

A Seattle University paper highlights the positive impact of ethical practices on business success.[352] The paper hints that companies with strong ethical labor practices can potentially experience increased employee retention and a boost in overall productivity. Furthermore, ethical companies are more likely to attract top talent and maintain a positive public image. As a result, this can lead to long-term business success.

However, adopting innovative policy solutions in the constantly changing mobility landscape can be difficult. Since startups emerge and automotive industries compete relentlessly to retain private vehicle ownership states for survival, adopting a proactive strategy is vital for progress.

As the landscape of transportation and employment continues to evolve, integrating advanced technologies and innovative business models holds the potential to further transform the industry. This transformation offers new ways to ensure job security and bolster economic stability for those operating within it. The rise of Mobility as a Service (MaaS) is a key driver of this change, leading to shifts in

---

[352]https://www.seattleu.edu/business/online/albers/blog/how-ethics-in-business-drive-success

vehicle ownership and usage patterns. These shifts not only promise to enhance operational efficiency but also pave the way for greater environmental sustainability.

In the face of such sweeping changes, effective leadership will play a critical role in shaping a mobile world that balances economic opportunity and technological innovation. As we move forward, it is essential to understand the type of leadership required to navigate this dynamic landscape and create a thriving, resilient future for all stakeholders.

Chapter 15
Leading in a Mobile World: Why Adaptability and Vision Matter More Than Ever

The digitized landscape of the mobility industry is expanding rapidly. This rapid advancement calls for effective leadership. Technological advancements and evolving consumer expectations mainly influence the passenger transportation sector. Therefore, it requires leaders who are adept at managing day-to-day operations and possess a forward-thinking mindset that can handle and leverage the changes.

The industry continues to evolve with innovations like autonomous vehicles (AVs) and integrated mobility solutions entering the passenger transportation markets. At the same time, the role of visionary leadership becomes essential in steering organizations toward sustainable success by using these innovations as efficiently and competitively as possible.

Leadership in the passenger transportation sector is somewhat more than traditional management practices. It involves adopting technological advancements and understanding market trends. Meanwhile, effective leadership in this sector also includes adapting to regulatory changes.

This dynamic environment demands leaders who can balance operational efficiency with strategic foresight. With that in mind, visionary leaders will be people who can anticipate future trends and align business strategies to address current challenges. This allows them to capitalize on emerging opportunities and drive their organizations through change. Furthermore, it also encourages innovation, a culture that supports growth.

One of the critical elements of effective leadership would be the ability to integrate technology into core business strategies. Take ride-hailing apps, for example. The advancements in autonomous driving and the development of Mobility as a Service (MaaS) platforms show us the role of technology in reshaping the transportation landscape.

Leaders must navigate these changes using technology to enhance service delivery, improve operational efficiency, and respond to evolving consumer preferences. Furthermore, an "abundance mindset" is essential in visionary leadership. This mindset encourages leaders to view challenges as opportunities for growth and collaboration rather than obstacles.

Visionary Leadership in the Passenger Transportation Sector

You would characterize visionary leadership as the ability to foresee future trends and emerging opportunities. It is also characterized by the ability to craft strategies that address present needs and anticipate and shape future developments. Such leadership involves inspiring a shared vision, aligning resources, and guiding an organization through transformative change.

A future-focused vision becomes essential when we talk about the passenger transportation sector. This is due to the need to adopt rapid technological advancements to meet shifting consumer behaviors and changing regulatory landscapes. The passenger transportation sector is a dynamic one. It is where innovation and disruption are constants, which makes a visionary leader's ability to anticipate and adapt to future trends a key component in determining an organization's success or failure.

For example, leaders who recognize the potential of electric vehicles, autonomous driving, and integrated mobility solutions are better positioned to drive their companies toward sustainable growth and competitive advantage. The main benefits of this approach are that it helps organizations to innovate continuously, stay relevant, and meet the emerging needs of consumers. Take Elon Musk's leadership at Tesla, for example.

Tesla has revolutionized the automotive industry by popularizing electric vehicles (EVs) and expanded its vision to include autonomous driving and sustainable energy solutions. Musk's approach integrates various elements of transportation innovation. It included the development of high-performance EVs and advancements in self-driving technology.

The company has influenced other automakers to accelerate their efforts in areas like EVs, AVs, and self-driving capabilities. Moreover, Tesla's success has helped to shift public perception of electric vehicles from niche products to mainstream options.

Technology as a Core Strategy in Modern Business Models

Incorporating technology as a core strategy is another essential factor in gaining a competitive edge in today's business environment. However, the scenario is more sophisticated and demanding in passenger transportation.

Technology enables companies to streamline operations and enhance customer experiences, among other advantages. It is the main driver behind innovation in the sector. For people transportation, this means utilizing technology to optimize everything from service availability and delivery to enhancing operational efficiency.

The recent tech advancements that are making monumental leaps in the sector have been AI, big data, and automation. These technologies have been central in shaping modern business models, including in the passenger transportation sector.

Organizations are gaining valuable insights into customer behavior, route optimization, efficient resource allocation, and service quality improvements through them. More importantly, these technologies have facilitated scalability to allow companies to expand their operations and reach new markets more efficiently.

We take Didi Chuxing as an example. It is one of China's leading ride-hailing services that uses a range of technological innovations to improve its metropolitan transportation service efficiency. The company has been using AI to optimize various aspects of its operations.[353] AI algorithms help the platform to match riders with drivers more efficiently.[354]

Didi Chuxing uses AI and automated machine learning algorithms to optimize routes and encourage carpooling through its platform. It has contributed positively to alleviating congestion in metropolitan areas. This approach potentially benefits individual users and contributes to broader city-wide traffic management strategies.[355]

The Adoption of Abundance Models in the Mobility Industry

An abundance mindset is a philosophy that believes ample opportunities and resources are available to everyone. We covered it in depth in the previous chapters. This mindset contrasts with a scarcity mentality in which it is assumed that

---

[353] https://www.slideshare.net/slideshow/how-chinese-company-didi-chuxing-uses-ai-machine-learning-to-revolutionize-transportation/124854272

[354] https://www.forbes.com/sites/bernardmarr/2018/11/26/ai-in-china-how-uber-rival-didi-chuxing-uses-machine-learning-to-revolutionize-transportation/

[355]https://www.unifr.ch/intman/en/assets/public/intman/files/news/2022_St udy_Sharing_Mobility_Economy_in_China_(DiDi%20Chuxing)_Simone%20 Ramseier.pdf

resources are limited and that one person's gain is necessarily another one's loss.

For business leaders, adopting an abundance mindset means focusing on creating opportunities and fostering collaboration while embracing the idea that collective success benefits all stakeholders. In the context of passenger transportation service development, innovation, and delivery, the advantages of an abundance mindset for business leaders can be numerous.

It can lead to increased partnerships and collaborations. Although competition in transportation would still exist, it would conform to an unconventional model of collaborative efforts to advance technology adoption and service optimization. Through this collaborative approach, business leaders in the mobility industry can innovate solutions and share success with leading organizations to move the industry forward.

Another significant implication of the abundance model in the passenger transportation sector is that when you consider endless possibilities, you are more inclined to experiment and innovate without fear of failure. However, this would depend on the individual organization's capabilities, and it can potentially create a culture of creativity and continuous improvement.

We will take the case of Lyft's collaborative consumption model to assess these benefits. We have analyzed the ride-sharing company in depth throughout previous chapters, but our focus is on the company's adoption and utilization of the abundance model.

John Zimmer and Logan Green founded the company to offer community-oriented ride-hailing services.[356] With its progression, Lyft started improving its market positioning through the abundance model. For instance, the company has built its brand around "ride-sharing" as a community service rather than just a transportation service.[357]

It emphasizes values like trust and safety to create a sense of community among drivers and riders. This focus on shared values has helped differentiate Lyft from its competitors. Lyft's abundance mindset has driven several innovative features like the Lyft Line (a carpooling option) and Lyft Scooters.[358] These innovations have been due to the company's belief in the potential for growth and improvement within the shared economy framework.

Acknowledging the Role of Collective Progress and Innovation

An abundance mindset can foster innovation by allowing leaders and teams to focus on collective progress rather than individual gain. This approach promotes collaboration and knowledge sharing. However, this requires individuals and

---

[356]https://www.brandcredential.com/post/the-effective-lyft-marketing-strategy-driving-success-in-the-ride-hailing-industry

[357]https://www.forbes.com/sites/simonmainwaring/2018/10/16/how-lyft-drives-growth-through-purpose/

[358] https://www.technologyreview.com/2015/10/13/10391/lyfts-search-for-a-new-mode-of-transport/

organizations to focus on collective success because that is when positive outcomes are most likely under the abundance model.

Take Google, which is popular for its innovative products and services. The tech giant has based its business on an abundance model. Google encourages employees to spend 20% of their time on personal projects, which has led to successful products like Gmail and Google News.[359] This policy demonstrates the company's belief in the boundless potential of its employees and their ideas.[360]

Analyzing Successful Leadership in the Mobility Industry

Agility and adaptability have been advantageous to the mobility industry. They have become core characteristics of successful organizations and companies in the industry. The ability to pivot quickly in response to market changes, consumer preferences, and technological advancements helps differentiate successful leaders from those struggling to keep pace.

This adaptability enables businesses to take advantage of new opportunities and emerging trends. It has been crucial in helping companies mitigate risks and maintain a competitive edge in the increasingly dynamic environment.

---

[359] https://www.cnbc.com/2021/12/16/google-20-percent-rule-shows-exactly-how-much-time-you-should-spend-learning-new-skills.html

[360] https://www.inc.com/bill-murphy-jr/google-says-it-still-uses-20-percent-rule-you-should-totally-copy-it.html

On the other hand, agility in leadership has been all about being proactive rather than reactive. It has encouraged industry leaders to anticipate trends and prepare their organizations to respond effectively to emerging challenges. It allowed companies to become resilient and adaptive and served as a foundation to navigate uncertainties within the industry.

These uncertainties were mainly due to cutting-edge innovations, novel organizational models, differentiated business models, and tech disruptions.

inDrive, formerly known as inDriver, is an international ride-hailing service that operates in over 749 cities across 46 countries, with more than 240 million app installations.[361]

Founded in 2013 and headquartered in Mountain View, California, inDrive has rapidly expanded its global presence, becoming the second most downloaded ride-hailing app worldwide in 2022 and 2023.

inDrive distinguishes itself from traditional ride-hailing platforms through its unique, user-centric approach of four dimensions:[362]

- **Fare Negotiation:** Unlike dominant conventional TNCs' services that set fares via algorithms, inDrive allows passengers to propose their own fare for a ride. Nearby drivers can then accept, decline, or

---

[361]https://indrive.com/en-us/company
[362]https://www.getwidget.dev/blog/the-business-model-and-revenue-generation-of-indriver/

counter the offer, facilitating a transparent and mutually agreeable pricing system.

- **Driver Autonomy:** Drivers have the freedom to choose rides based on proposed fares and their own preferences, without facing penalties for declining requests. This flexibility empowers drivers to make decisions that best suit their schedules and financial goals.

- **No Surge Pricing:** inDrive does not implement surge pricing during peak times, ensuring that passengers are not subjected to inflated fares during high-demand periods.

- **Community-Centric Approach:** The platform emphasizes building trust and reliability by allowing users to view mutual contacts with drivers, enhancing safety and fostering a sense of community.

This innovative model offers passengers more control over ride costs and provides drivers with greater autonomy, setting inDrive apart in the competitive ride-hailing industry.[363]

---

[363]https://www.logisticsmiddleeast.com/transport/breaking-the-algorithm-how-indrives-democratic-model-empowers-drivers-and-riders

The Growing Environment of Continuous Learning and Innovation

Business leaders must develop a culture where continuous learning and innovation help the organization stay ahead of the curve. This approach is necessary for fostering an environment where employees seek new knowledge, experiment with new ideas, and continuously improve their skills. We learned from Google's example above how dedicating time to personal projects could also lead to significant product and service solutions.

Leaders who prioritize learning and innovation create dynamic workplaces where creativity flourishes. It also gives way to an environment where employees are motivated to contribute to the company's success. However, an organization must implement several key strategies to cultivate such a culture.

For instance, leaders will have to promote a growth mindset where employees are encouraged to view challenges as opportunities for development rather than obstacles. This will provide opportunities for professional development, such as training programs and mentorship, which will help employees stay current with industry trends and enhance their skills.

Additionally, leaders can create channels for idea-sharing and feedback to allow employees to contribute to innovation and process improvements.

Jeff Bezos, the founder of Amazon, implemented the principles of continuous learning and innovation.[364] Under Bezos's leadership, Amazon has become a global leader in e-commerce and technology through experimentation and customer-centricity.[365] Bezos's approach to leadership also involved fostering a culture that valued experimentation and learning from failures.[366]

Amazon encourages its employees to take risks and test new ideas, often leading to groundbreaking innovations like the Amazon Web Services (AWS) and the Kindle.[367] The company operates with a "Day 1" mentality where employees are encouraged to approach each day with the same entrepreneurial spirit as when the company was founded.[368] This mindset drives continuous improvement and ensures that the company remains agile and responsive to market changes.

The impact of this emphasis on innovation is evident in Amazon's sustained growth and market leadership. The company has been evolving its offerings and embracing new technologies. This has allowed Amazon to remain dominant

---

[364]https://www.researchgate.net/publication/322187038_Multi-dimensional_nature_of_innovation_at_Amazon

[365]https://keeganedwards.com/demystifying-jeff-bezos-business-strategy-the-driving-force-behind-amazons-success/

[366]https://cdotimes.com/2024/05/23/amazon-case-study-lessons-from-jeff-bezos-leadership-and-innovation/

[367] https://www.sciencedirect.com/science/article/pii/S0160791X19301022

[368]https://www.forbes.com/sites/quora/2017/04/21/what-is-jeff-bezos-day-1-philosophy/

in multiple sectors, including retail, cloud computing, and artificial intelligence.

The Effective Strategy of Empowering Teams for Effective Leadership

Empowering teams is also a key component of effective leadership, and it often plays a crucial role in building organizational resilience. Resilient teams are better equipped to handle challenges and adapt to changes. Moreover, they can maintain high performance under pressure thanks to motivation and encouragement from senior leadership.

It is also important to mention that empowering teams involves equipping them with the necessary resources, authority, and support to make decisions and drive outcomes. One way to do that is to create an organizational culture where trust and autonomy are key values.

This includes participation from business leaders who delegate authority and trust their teams to make decisions. As a result, it creates a sense of ownership and accountability. While this approach can boost morale, it can also increase team members' confidence.

However, it also requires leaders to set clear goals and freely allow autonomy. This helps employees determine how to achieve their goals, leading to greater creativity and innovation. Furthermore, regular feedback and recognition of achievements can reinforce a sense of empowerment and encourage ongoing development.

Investing in professional development is one of the most effective techniques for building resilient teams. Training programs, mentorship opportunities, and career development resources can help team members develop new skills. What's more interesting is that it helps keep them engaged with their work. It is an investment in personal growth that contributes to a more capable and motivated workforce.

This time, we take Satya Nadella's leadership at Microsoft as a compelling case study in transforming company culture to focus on growth and learning.[369] When Nadella became CEO in 2014, Microsoft was seen as a stagnant giant struggling with internal friction.[370] Nadella's vision was to shift the company's culture toward one that embraced a "growth mindset." The ultimate goal of this approach was to emphasize continuous learning and collaboration.[371]

Microsoft underwent significant cultural changes as he promoted values like empathy and inclusivity.[372] In addition, he increased the focus on innovation, contributing to a more dynamic and resilient workforce.

We learn that a supportive company culture can enhance employee engagement, performance, and innovation. This is

---

[369]https://publishing.london.edu/cases/satya-nadella-at-microsoft-instilling-a-growth-mindset/

[370]https://www.cnbc.com/2024/02/04/microsoft-ceo-satya-nadella-hits-10-year-anniversary.html

[371]https://www.nytimes.com/2024/07/14/technology/microsoft-ai-satya-nadella.html

[372]https://www.cnbc.com/2018/07/17/how-microsoft-has-evolved-under-satya-nadella.html

because employees are more likely to be motivated when they feel valued and supported. This ultimately translates into higher productivity and commitment at work.

A positive work environment fosters collaboration and creativity. It also creates a strong sense of belonging, which drives organizational success. It is worth noting that a key aspect of a supportive culture is open communication.

Organizations that encourage transparent communication create an environment where employees feel comfortable sharing their ideas and concerns. Regular check-ins, feedback sessions, and open-door policies contribute to a culture of trust and respect. It often leads to recognition and celebration of achievements to reinforce a positive atmosphere and motivate employees to strive for excellence.

When we consider these strategies in the context of the passenger transportation sector, we can understand the value of visionary leadership and technology integration as key to organizational success. The role of the abundance model is also among the critical factors that can help organizations in the mobility industry achieve sustained success and drive innovation.

As we move toward the conclusion of this exploration into the evolving mobility landscape, it is clear that effective leadership in the passenger transportation sector transcends traditional management practices. Visionary leaders who can anticipate trends, adapt to rapid technological advancements, and foster cultures of innovation and resilience have become indispensable. The transformative role of technology integration, abundance models, and collaborative approaches have shown how organizations can navigate change, remain competitive, and meet evolving consumer demands. These leaders, equipped with strategic foresight and a commitment to collective growth, are redefining success in a dynamic, digitally-driven industry. In the concluding chapter, we will synthesize these insights and provide a pathway forward for thriving in the future of mobility.

Chapter 16
Key Takeaways and Why They Matter for the Future of Mobility

A combination of technological innovations with a shift in consumer behaviors and government policies now determines the future of the mobility industry. However, there have been countless trends and innovations with long-term implications.

We already have discussed many of those trends throughout the book. We also examined the potential scenario where these trends merge in the metropolitan and rural transportation environments. Transportation is approaching a wave of major technological innovation with an increased focus on sustainability.

To thrive as a leader in the mobility industry, there are three essential guidelines that demand attention, vision, and a commitment to progress. These principles illuminate the path for any organization aiming to lead in this transformative era and empower leaders to seize the full potential of a rapidly evolving landscape.

First, the future of mobility is Electric, Autonomous, Personalized, and Connected. The mobility industry stands on the brink of unprecedented change, driven by breakthroughs in electrification, autonomy, personalization, and connectivity. To lead successfully, you must understand that these elements are not mere trends; they are the building blocks of tomorrow's transportation systems. Electric vehicles promise a cleaner and more sustainable future, while autonomous technologies revolutionize how we move, enabling greater safety, efficiency, and convenience. Personalization transforms the passenger experience, ensuring every journey is uniquely tailored to meet individual needs. Finally, connectivity ties it all together, fostering real-time communication, predictive insights, and seamless service integration. Thriving leaders will not merely adapt to these shifts—they will be the architects of change, leveraging each pillar to redefine how people connect, travel, and live.

Second, no market is taken for granted for dominant Transportation Network Company (TNC) providers when leaders' business strategies are user-centric. InDrive serves as a powerful testament to this principle. In today's competitive environment, consumer expectations evolve faster than ever, and complacency is the enemy of growth. Leaders must embrace a user-centric approach, where every decision is shaped by the needs, preferences, and experiences of those they serve. InDrive's disruptive model exemplifies this by placing fare negotiation, driver autonomy, and community trust at the forefront. By empowering users and listening to their voices, it has proven that even established markets can be upended by innovation. As a leader, your strategy must place customers at its core, recognizing that the key to winning loyalty and market share lies in genuine connection, responsiveness, and respect for individual needs.

Third, what brought your business success over the last 20 years will not enable you to thrive in the new digital economy of the future. The pace of change in the mobility sector is relentless, driven by technological advances, shifting consumer expectations, and an increasingly interconnected world. What worked in the past—a reliance on established practices, rigid structures, and legacy models—will no longer suffice in this dynamic ecosystem. Thriving leaders recognize that yesterday's success stories must give way to a forward-looking mindset that embraces change, experimentation, and continuous reinvention. You must be willing to challenge assumptions, pivot quickly, and remain agile in response to new opportunities and challenges. The leaders who will shape the future are those who welcome disruption with open arms and see reinvention not as a risk but as a pathway to greater resilience, relevance, and growth.

As a Passenger Transportation provider—whether private or government—it is critical to establish your "why" before taking any actions. When you clearly define the purpose that drives your organization, every subsequent decision gains clarity and impact. Your "why" should act as the North Star, guiding every strategy, operation, and collaboration. In this post-digital economy, thriving leaders understand that purpose goes beyond profits; it encompasses a commitment to providing exceptional, sustainable, and transformative transportation experiences. To operate and grow effectively in the new economy, adopting an abundant model becomes crucial. As discussed in Chapter 11, this approach calls for embracing open ecosystems and forging strong partnerships with like-minded entities that share your cultural values and vision. This alignment of purpose ensures your organization operates as part of a tribe of doers—those who are proud to be on the journey and who foster open collaboration. To achieve this, leaders must cultivate new management skills and assemble diverse profiles that reflect the evolving demands of the industry.

The transition within the passenger transportation sector from mere trips to enriched, hospitality-driven experiences underscores the need for an abundant mindset. This is not just about implementing new technologies but orchestrating a well-trained and empowered team that works in harmony to deliver unparalleled experiences. By aligning every member of your organization with the "why," you create a culture of purpose that drives outstanding outcomes. To achieve this, leaders must define, communicate, and continuously reinforce abundant Key Performance Indicators (KPIs). These KPIs should reflect not only operational goals but also a shared commitment to innovation, sustainability, and customer-centric excellence. In this transformational journey, the "why" anchors every action, while the "what" and "how" provide structure and execution. A clearly articulated purpose, paired with daily communication and embodiment of these principles, becomes a powerful driver of change and growth.

Embracing new technologies is not merely an option but a necessity; it is the cornerstone for achieving accelerated growth in any passenger transportation endeavor. As the industry evolves, technological innovations drive efficiency, enhance the customer experience, and open up new opportunities for growth.

There is ongoing integration of electric vehicles, autonomous vehicles, and sustainable mobility solutions in the industry. These innovations will redefine passenger transportation in ways that improve efficiency, safety, and environmental impact in most transportation models.

Autonomous Vehicles will potentially be one of the most considerable technologies in advance for transportation with their excellent sensors and artificial intelligence models. Such vehicles will transform transportation by improving safety records, decreasing congestion, and increasing efficiency. As AV technology becomes more advanced, human errors will decrease. This could lead to less accidents and a smoother flow of traffic.

Widespread use of AVs could increase the ease of access to transportation for more people, including the older population and those with disabilities. Meanwhile, the transition to electric vehicles will lead to further reductions in maintenance costs, the emission of greenhouse gases, and our reliance on fossil fuels. The EVs are now a practical solution in daily life with the advancement in battery technology, further facilitated by the current innovation of new EVs with longer ranges and shorter recharging times. Similarly, with charging infrastructure development and lower costs, EVs could soon become the new normal in personalized and public transport.

At the same time, Mobility as a Service (MaaS) platforms are changing how users can access and manage their travel experience. A MaaS platform integrates multiple modes of transport—buses, trains, bikes, livery and ride-hailing services—into a unified and user-friendly platform. It requires people to plan and pay for their trips in one service. It makes the transportation experience easier. Over time, MaaS could become the backbone of metropolitan mobility and influence the industry. As a result, it can reduce the need to own vehicles and significantly reduce traffic congestion.

The future of transportation will also evolve between metropolitan and rural settings, mainly determined by population density, infrastructure development, and technological adoption. Integrating AVs, EVs, eVTOLs and MaaS platforms in a metropolitan environment will likely lead to more efficient and sustainable transportation operations.

Technologies in smart cities, like intelligent traffic management, will also lead to efficiency in transportation networks. For instance, intelligent traffic signals reduce the delays faced by commuters. Meanwhile, expanding electric share bikes and shared mobility options will also support sustainable urban transportation. The process is expected to speed up with the availability of dedicated lanes for AVs and EVs and 3D flight paths for eVTOLs, increasing safety and efficiency.

On the other hand, new transportation technologies bring various benefits to rural areas, which will also benefit from multiple technologies. However, the effect might be slower as rural environments face different challenges. Since the population density and infrastructural development are low, adopting AVs, EVs, and eVTOLs in rural areas can delay public transportation improvements. However, it promises to improve connectivity, the reach of rural communities, and a significant reconfiguration of metropolitan zones in the long run.

The autonomous shuttles and on-demand ride services provide additional transportation options. Building EV charging networks in rural regions will allow for quickly increasing adoption of electric vehicles and sustainable practices. Then, we have policies and government regulations that will be instrumental in shaping the future of mobility.

We are looking forward to policies that will support innovation and investments in infrastructure technology. These investments will broaden the research and development space to tackle safety and accessibility challenges in the mobility landscape.

In the future, a range of policies could encourage EV uptake. In the same way, the regulation of testing and deployment of AVs and eVTOLs will help to transit rapidly to new transportation technologies. Furthermore, effective policy frameworks will ensure the benefits of these improvements are widely distributed and contribute to society's overall goals.

In addition, technological advances will continue changing transportation. Innovation in AI, data analytics, and connectivity will bring ways to provide more efficient and personalized services in transportation. For example, connected vehicles will communicate with one another, and the smart infrastructure to optimize traffic flow and reduce accidents.

The smart infrastructure with developments like intelligent traffic signals will boost the efficiency of real-time traffic monitoring systems. In turn, it will also lead to higher safety in transportation networks. Continuous research in evolving technologies, including hyperloop systems and advanced battery solutions, could shift how consumers approach and utilize transportation facilities. For that reason, consumer preferences will be a crucial factor in determining the future of personal mobility solutions in metropolitan and rural environments.

Consumers are becoming more aware of the environmental and economic concerns of mobility and transportation solutions. This could further drive the adoption and awareness regarding emerging technologies, like EVs, AVs, eVTOLs, and MaaS. Due to that, modern transportation systems will be improved in efficiency, sustainability, and integration. It will bring ease of traveling with greater accessibility and affordability with favorable policies from the government.

This technological progress will allow instant coordination between the different transportation modes, assisting users in planning and executing their journey effectively. Integrated platforms will offer personalized travel suggestions, optimized routes, and payments. All are facilitated through a single user interface. All of that will potentially enhance convenience and make it effortless for people to move around daily.

Sustainability will remain a significant factor in determining the passenger transportation sector's future. It is the main factor that led to the rise of electric and autonomous vehicles, which are now in consideration for mass and personal adoption. It will be tremendously helpful in cutting greenhouse gas emissions and improving energy efficiency. As a result, more effective sustainable practices will emerge in the passenger transportation sector.

The connectivity will improve autonomous and electric vehicle efficiency thanks to an evolving interconnected ecosystem. These vehicles will communicate with existing infrastructure in smart cities to optimize traffic routes through effective route planning. Consequently, it will reduce the risk of road accidents and traffic congestion.

Meanwhile, developments like high-speed transportation systems (e.g., hyperloop systems) could connect smart cities for long-distance travel. As a result, long-distance commutes would be faster and more efficient. Despite all that, equitable access to transportation facilities and innovative mobility models will be the main success-driving factor.

It will effectively address the general disparities between localities, communities, and large population groups. This will play into the success of cutting-edge mobility solutions that expand transit options sustainably and effectively. It will involve developing infrastructure and transportation systems (and networks) focused on equitable access.

The future of mobility holds exciting possibilities for passenger transportation providers and all its stakeholders. Technological advancements and shifting consumer preferences drive it. Thanks to public-private collaborations, these factors are also driving supportive policy frameworks. We will focus on creating a more sustainable, equitable and accessible transportation system that matches our changing world.